A Different Kind of Fast

Praise for *A Different Kind of Fast: Feeding Our True Hungers in Lent*

"In *A Different Kind of Fast*, Christine Valters Paintner takes readers on a transformative pilgrimage of self-discovery and spiritual growth. With wisdom and grace, she unveils our deep yearning for our true home in God and offers a treasure trove of practices and guidance to nourish our souls. Reading this book is like sitting at the feet of a modern-day desert mother, who, with wisdom and care, guides us on our way. I wholeheartedly recommend *A Different Kind of Fast* to anyone seeking a profound Lenten experience or simply desiring to feel closer to God."

—**Adam Bucko**, author of *Let Your Heartbreak Be Your Guide: Lessons in Engaged Contemplation*

"Christine Valters Paintner has a wonderful gift for inviting us to meet traditional spiritual practices in new and expansive ways. *A Different Kind of Fast* is both a deeply nourishing revisioning of fasting and a new, beautiful, and insightful approach to the season of Lent. It's perfect for everyone, whether you are new to Lent or have a long relationship with this season of prayer."

—**Carl McColman**, author of *The New Big Book of Christian Mysticism* and *Eternal Heart*

"In a time when consumerist pressure weighs heavily on all of us, Christine Valters Paintner's *A Different Kind of Fast* asks us to consider what 'giving something up' for Lent really means. Drawing on the wisdom of the desert mothers and fathers and their contemporary descendants, this book offers readers a multisensory approach to contemplation that is sensitive, thoughtful, and inclusive."

—**Kaya Oakes**, author of *The Defiant Middle* and *Radical Reinvention*

"This insightful book will help open doors for spiritual directors they may not have anticipated. Highly recommended!"

—**Rev. Seifu Singh-Molares**, executive director, Spiritual Directors International

A
Different
Kind *of* Fast

feeding our true
hungers *in* lent

CHRISTINE
VALTERS
PAINTNER

ILLUSTRATIONS
BY KREG YINGST

Broadleaf Books
Minneapolis

A DIFFERENT KIND OF FAST
Feeding Our True Hungers in Lent

30 29 28 27 26 25 24   2 3 4 5 6 7 8 9

Illustrations © 2022 Kreg Yingst

Library of Congress Cataloging-in-Publication Data

Names: Paintner, Christine Valters, author. | Yingst, Kreg, illustrator.
Title: A different kind of fast : feeding our true hungers in Lent / [by
   Christine Valters Paintner] ; illustrations by Kreg Yingst.
Description: Minneapolis, MN : Broadleaf Books, [2024] | Includes
   bibliographical references.
Identifiers: LCCN 2023014885 (print) | LCCN 2023014886 (ebook) | ISBN
   9781506492117 (print) | ISBN 9781506492124 (ebook)
Subjects: LCSH: Lent. | Fasting--Religious aspects--Christianity.
Classification: LCC BV85 .P26 2024 (print) | LCC BV85 (ebook) | DDC
   242/.34--dc23/eng/20230630
LC record available at https://lccn.loc.gov/2023014885
LC ebook record available at https://lccn.loc.gov/2023014886

Cover design: Studio Gearbox
Cover image: shutterstock_2201386045

Print ISBN: 978-1-5064-9211-7
eBook ISBN: 978-1-5064-9212-4

Contents

Contents

Why spend your money for what is not bread,
your wages for what fails to satisfy.
Heed me and you shall delight in rich fare,
come to me heedfully that you may have life.

Isaiah 55:2–3

Introduction

What are the things you hunger for?

I don't mean cravings like your favorite meal or drink, or the obsessive scrolling through our social media accounts we can sometimes get caught up in, which often fuels our anxiety over the world or our sense of the inadequacy of our lives.

These things are not ultimately nourishing. What is nourishing are the things that are life-giving, joy-bringing, peace-arising, purpose-revealing.

We live in a culture that depends on distracting us from our true hungers, because when we identify with these surface hungers we will consume more and more in the search for satisfaction.

You may have a long practice of Lenten reflection or you may be new to the season. Either way I want to invite you into a different kind of fast, one which helps you identify those patterns and habits that distract you from the fullness of life and open up space for the feast that awaits each of us.

This past year has been for me a long season of release. Ongoing health issues can bring clarity over what is most important in a given season of life. The word that chose me for the new year to focus on is *distillation*, and it provides a compass for how I discern what to take on and what to let go of.

While there has been some clearing out of closets and donations to the charity shop, most of what I am releasing are the old patterns and ways of being that deplete me and obstruct my full access to the divine image carved into my heart.

A few weeks ago, I found a piece of paper with three things written on it. It must have been part of a ritual I participated in, but I cannot remember the details. But the three things were all habits in my life I felt called to surrender, to no longer carry the weight of. Things like a sense of over-responsibility that developed early in childhood from growing up in an alcoholic home, the weight of burdens I carry, some of which are my own and some of which feel ancestral, and my fears of scarcity that often reemerge, especially when my health is challenged.

I smiled because I had been reading through some old journals from the last two years in preparation for a burning ritual I have been doing regularly (another ritual of release). As I reread, I spend time and really pay attention to the wisdom gleaned from those rambling reflections and I notice my patterns. I had seen those patterns named above repeating themselves in the pages of my journal as well. The longings for more trust, more rest, more ease.

As I was cleaning out the closet in my office, I found three large stones. Each was about double the size of my palm and I had gathered them over time. I knew these were arriving to me as gift, as symbols of the weight I carry, and I knew I had to release them.

There is a beautiful poem from Rainer Maria Rilke in which he writes: "Fear not the sorrow you feel, give your weight back to the earth, for heavy are the mountains, heavy the seas." It is a quote I have carried with me for years. In those moments when grief and longing and overwhelm feel like too much to carry, it reminds me to return to wild places and offer whatever burden I am carrying back to the land and sea. Earth and ocean can bear the weight of our grief, our compulsions, our life-denying habits.

I went out to Rusheen Bay in Galway with my three large stones. I found a quiet place by the water and sat on a rock by the edge for a long while. I started by praying for loved ones, for my friend whose husband died recently, for my sweet dog who was having surgery that day to remove a tumor, for my aunt whose death last year continues to grieve me, for my own health, and then for the happenings in the world that continue to break my heart.

Finally, when I was ready, I took each stone in my hand one by one. I held it, I felt its textures and weight. I named the burden I had been carrying which it symbolized. And then I heaved it into the bay, asking Spirit; the angels, saints, and ancestors; and the land and sea to hold it, to transmute and transform it. I did this three times, each time watching the splash of the stone into water and seeing the circles rippling outward. I know when we keep working to heal ourselves, the healing impacts others in ways we cannot see.

I sat for a long time in the silence that followed, feeling lighter in my being. In the space I opened up inside me, gratitude came rushing in, along with a sense of joy at this moment of clarity. I knew those burdens kept me from the fullness of life, and this was another step on my own journey of healing, which is the work of a lifetime.

What are the things you are holding onto? What are the patterns and ways of being, the habits and compulsions that are life-depleting? Which things divert your attention again and again from the radiant creation that you are? Are there resentments? Overwork? Grief denied? Are you a member of a marginalized group repeatedly hearing on the news how your life is less valuable?

And what are the true hungers you experience in quiet moments when you have a chance to pause and listen?

Lent is a six-and-a-half-week season of renewed spiritual practice, inspired by Jesus's forty days in the desert spent fasting and praying. If you're part of the Christian tradition, you may have some kind of food you give up for the season as a way to be more mindful and in solidarity with those who hunger for food and shelter.

This book invites you into a different kind of fast, however. Physical fasting from various kinds of consuming in a world oversaturated with things can be valuable. But ultimately, they point us to other things in our lives that numb us out with distraction or heighten our anxiety and fearfulness.

In the pages ahead you will be invited into a series of nonphysical fasts where we explore what it means to fast from multitasking, anxiety, rushing, holding it all together, planning, and certainty and instead to embrace presence, abundance, slowness, tenderness, unfolding, and mystery.

Our human patterns of grasping and avoiding are part of who we are as beings with limitations. Fasting can be a way of temporarily trying to remove something that feels compulsive or not life-giving in favor of embracing something that does deeply nourish.

I invite you to not just try to identify and set aside these ways of being, which restrict the fullness of life, but to also actively embrace and feast upon the rich spiritual nourishment available to us.

These forty days are a sacred journey through the wilderness, which means there will be moments of challenge. Even if we live in the middle of the suburbs or in the heart of the city, the wilderness becomes a metaphor for those places we need to wrestle and ultimately soften toward ourselves, bring lavish compassion to the things we struggle with, and listen for ancient wisdom to practice our way into a renewed way of being.

You may wonder if a forty-day retreat is even possible for you in the midst of work commitments, family, and other things that demand your time and energy. Contemplative theologian Barbara Holmes writes that she is convinced "that contemplation can occur anywhere; stained glass windows and desert retreats are not necessary." In fact, she continues, our times of "duress may facilitate the turn inward." Often it is precisely in those seasons of life when we are stretched thin, feeling overwhelmed, and completely vulnerable that our hearts start to dig a little deeper within ourselves to encounter the loving presence of what the mystics have told us is the divine spark within each of us.

In the second and third centuries these radical women and men sought out wilderness places for simplicity and to fast from their compulsions in service of cultivating greater love for the divine and the world.

Later in our journey you will be meditating with this story from Amma Syncletica, one of the desert mothers, who makes it clear that it is our intention, rather than our location, that makes all the difference:

> *Amma Syncletica said, "There are many who live in the mountains and behave as if they were in town, and they are wasting their time. It is possible to be a solitary in one's mind while living in a crowd, and it is possible for one who is a solitary to live in the crowd of his own thoughts." (Syncletica 19)*

The ammas and abbas of the desert were clear that simply going off on retreat in silence and solitude does not automatically mean we will find inner stillness. In fact, many seek this kind of experience and yet their thoughts are filled with chatter, worry, and distraction. And similarly, those who live in the cities can cultivate a loving presence to each moment so that they find stillness no matter what is happening around them.

Similarly, Barbara Holmes reinforces this idea that the desert is not required to have a wilderness experience:

> *Today's wilderness can be found in bustling suburban*
> *and urban centers, on death row, in homeless shelters*
> *in the middle of the night, in the eyes of a hospice*
> *patient, and in the desperation of AIDS orphans*
> *in Africa and around the world. Perhaps these are*
> *the postmodern desert mothers and fathers. Perhaps*
> *contemplative spaces can be found wherever people*
> *skirt the margins of inclusion. Perhaps those whom*
> *we value least have the most to teach.*

We might be tempted to think that if only life could slow down and we could have a period of retreat, then we could cultivate our spiritual life. But our wisdom teachers are clear: the wilderness is right in our midst and our invitation is to practice here and now.

My own ritual that emerged with the stones was the culmination of many years of reflection and practice and, to be clear, I am still on that journey. Releasing those stones was not an act of magic to lift my struggles from me. It was an act of trust in forces greater than myself, Spirit and the land, to help sustain me in directing my attention toward what is more life-giving.

In a culture that has everything available to us 24/7, it can feel like an act of deprivation to give up certain things. Yet what I keep discovering is that in a world glutted by choice, my heart feels more at peace in releasing what is not necessary and in fact weighs me down or numbs me out.

Ultimately, the practice of fasting is about making more space within us to encounter our deepest, most radiant selves. How do we listen to the whispers of the Holy One when we constantly distract ourselves with social media and doom-scrolling? How do we discover the radical abundance available to us, not of food or entertainment, but of nourishing gifts like joy, peace, love, and gratitude? How do we make room for the grief inside us, which is a witness to how much we have loved, if we are fighting to be strong and keep control in an unpredictable world?

One of the issues I have always had with Lenten fasting, though, is that it seems to have become for many a second chance at new year's resolutions. Fasting from chocolate is not a bad thing in itself, but if we approach it from a diet mentality or a sense of shame about eating certain foods, then we are not in the spirit of fasting as a spiritual practice. In fact, for those of us with a history of any kind of disordered eating, fasting can trigger our need to eat the "correct way"—whatever that might mean for you. This kind of fasting is merely an extension of the cultural mindset of body shame and control.

In this journey we will make together in the coming weeks, I invite you to release the deprivation mindset as much as possible. It is not by eating as little as possible or denying ourselves that we transform and grow in holiness. Fasting is ultimately a paradox of emptying out to be filled, paring back to receive a different kind of feast, one that nourishes our true hungers. Our fast is an act of discernment of the habits that keep us from this rich feast available to us.

What I find fascinating in Thomas Ryan's *The Sacred Art of Fasting* is his description of fasting as being marked not by deprivation as much as preparation:

> *The Hebrews, the Aramaeans, the Arabs, and the Ethiopians all used the same word for fasting, a word that appears in both early and late Hebrew Bible writings: tsoum. In modern Hebrew the word is Ta'anit. The word in its first level of meaning signifies "withholding all natural food from the body," especially for a religious purpose. The second level of meaning includes an expression of sorrow for sins and a penitential offering. Together they convey the idea of voluntary deprivation of the bodily appetites for the purpose of orienting the human spirit to God. The two "summit" experiences in the Hebrew scriptures of encounters with God are those of Moses and Elijah. For both, the encounter took place on Mount Sinai*

> *and was preceded by a fast of forty days and forty*
> *nights—on the mountain covered in a cloud for*
> *Moses (Exod. 34:28) and in the desert for Elijah*
> *(1 Kings 19:8). For each, the fast was marked by a*
> *spirit of preparation.*

Fasting helps us to orient ourselves toward the Holy One. Throughout Hebrew and Christian Scripture we meet those witnesses to this practice as essential to their own journeys of transformation and profound encounter, including Moses, Elijah, and Jesus. We see the practice as fundamentally an act of humility, where we remember our humanness and understand what our deepest needs are.

Fasting can help us to remember our true hunger. At heart, the act of fasting is about growing in relationship to the sacred presence. Experiencing hunger gets us in touch with the desire for something we do not have. It is the longing for it and our deep need. But we can get overwhelmed by our hungers for things, especially in a culture that worships consumerism and in which the divide between rich and poor grows ever wider. Stepping back from this helps us to see what we are really yearning for in our lives.

I think of my habit of clearing off my desk and filing away old papers when I am starting on a new project. If I prolong this task it may slip into procrastination, but the impulse and desire is to remove some of the external clutter, which creates a sense of inner spaciousness as well.

The outer clutter and inner clutter are often reflections of each other. I have fewer distractions from the project I want to be working on, and it makes it a more satisfying process for me. I find this too when I rearrange the furniture in a room: I suddenly get a new perspective. Fasting can create breathing space for a new perspective on our lives. We have been so used to looking at things a certain way, we discover with small shifts there is so much more beneath the surface awaiting our attention.

Fasting from foods is only one kind of fast. There are many other kinds too. We can fast from acquiring more "things," and excessive consumption, as the physical and material realm, as with the materiality of food, and how we understand it, limit it, or explore it differently, becomes a portal to the spiritual. We may find that cleaning the house and preparing a beautiful meal lend themselves to celebratory occasions—different kinds of fasting—and help to lift us from the mundane moments to open us to a deeper connection with God.

In a world where the sacred is infused into the material world, what we release on the physical realm can also impact our interior life. Fasting is preparation, which means clearing out a space for something new to enter.

Fasting isn't only connected to a physical level. We can also fast from thoughts and patterns in our lives that are life-denying. Fasting creates space in our lives for other—life-giving—thoughts to emerge. Rather than feeling jostled about by so many conflicting internal thoughts or tasks, when we fast we make room internally for something else, and we are able to breathe more deeply.

In the Hebrew Scriptures, the prophet Isaiah speaks about fasting as profoundly connected to transformation, both personal and cultural. When we release our life-denying habits and thoughts, we discover a new freedom to live differently. This is an internal freedom not dictated by outer circumstances. Ultimately this internal freedom leads us to desire for liberation for all beings and Isaiah makes this connection to justice:

> *Is not this the fast that I choose: to loose the bonds*
> *of injustice, to undo the thongs of the yoke, to let*
> *the oppressed go free, and to break every yoke? Is it*
> *not to share your bread with the hungry, and bring*
> *the homeless poor into your house; when you see the*
> *naked, to cover them, and not to hide yourself from*
> *your own kin? (Isaiah 58:6–7 (NRSV))*

As this wisdom text reveals, fasting helps reveal our true hunger and the hunger of others. And in the process of discovering this, we begin to see what is life-giving for us as intimately intertwined with the well-being of the entire Earth community. We don't fast merely for personal transformation, although this is a step along the way. We fast to widen our vision on ourselves and ultimately to connect to our longings to bring conditions of freedom for all.

Not only does fasting connect us to our true hunger, it has a way of also attuning us to the greater mystery in which we, as the book of Acts says, "live and move and have our being" (17:28). Thomas Ryan deepens our understanding of how fasting functions, writing:

> *Fasting as a religious act increases our sensitivity to*
> *that mystery always and everywhere present to us.*
> *It is a passageway into the world of spirit to explore*
> *its territory and bring back a wisdom necessary for*
> *living a fulfilled life. It is an invitation to awareness,*
> *a call to compassion for the needy, a cry of distress*
> *and a song of joy. It is a discipline of self-restraint, a*
> *ritual of purification, and a sanctuary for offerings*
> *of atonement.*

I love this litany of the fruits of fasting. When we fast, we make space to see the sacred thresholds shimmering everywhere we go. It brings us more fully present to the world and to those in need. It helps us to heal our wounds and creates room for joy. Atonement is a process of removing obstacles between ourselves and God. Fasting is an intentional way of removing those things that lead us further away.

I am sometimes asked how we know if we have an authentic encounter with the divine and my answer is always love. When our hearts are expanded and we start to see our fellow living beings as worthy of our care, then we know the sacred has been moving in our hearts.

One of the early teachings of the Christian church I find helpful to understand fasting is from John Cassian. Cassian, an early theologian, writes about what he calls the three renunciations. Renunciations are an intentional giving up of certain patterns or ways of being in the world and one form fasting can take. For Cassian, the first renunciation is of our former way of life and shifting our focus to our heart's deep desire. He assumes his listeners have perhaps become too invested in pleasing others, in achievements, or other externally focused motivations for how we live. By beginning to intentionally turn our attention inward, we listen for the way the sacred pulses in our own hearts call us to live from this holy direction.

The second renunciation, Cassian says, is giving up our mindless thoughts. Our minds are full of chatter all the time: judgments about ourselves and others, fears and anxieties over the future, overwhelm at world issues, the stress of illness, stories we tell about our lives, regrets over the past, imagined conversations with others, and more. It can be exhausting to follow all these trails of anxiousness. Intentional thought and meditative practice have always been about calming the mind so that the spirit can listen to another, deeper, truer voice. In the beginning we may need to start by focusing our thoughts on an object of attention, as in centering prayer where we choose a sacred word to bring our awareness back to the divine. As we continue this practice, however, we eventually may find ourselves not needing to focus thoughts anymore, but simply listening to the heart's wisdom. We begin by making the conscious choice to listen by quieting and clearing out the babble and prattle of our minds so that the heart's shimmering can become the focus.

The third renunciation I find the most powerful. We are called to renounce even our images of God so that we can meet God in the fullness of that divine reality beyond the boxes and limitations we create. So many of us have inherited harmful images of God taught by others that are not fruitful to our flourishing. Images of a judgmental God, a vending-machine God, a capricious God, a prosperity God, a God made in the image of whiteness. We project our human experiences onto the divine. This is a natural impulse, but our soul's deepening depends upon our freeing ourselves from these limiting images so we might have an encounter with the face of the sacred in all of its expansiveness and possibility. We might feel called to fast from these life-denying images to open our hearts to something wider.

We do not have to retreat to the desert or join a monastery to find this path of deepened intimacy with God. We each have the opportunity to choose this inner work of discerning what we hold onto and what we release at every season of our lives. We each have the choice to make. Sometimes this kind of radical simplicity accompanies a move, for example, when downsizing from a family home to an apartment. Sometimes we are forced by circumstance to change our outer life, perhaps due to illness or taking care of a sick parent. This exterior transformation is not a necessary prerequisite for the inner transformation we are all called to seek.

One of the beautiful aspects of the Christian liturgical cycle is that the call to reflection and intensified spiritual practice returns again and again each year and meets us wherever we are. The purpose of these acts of letting go is always in service of love. When we fast out of a misplaced sense of competition or a diet mentality, we lose this focus and it becomes something that distorts reality rather than clarifies it.

When we fast, we stand humbly in the presence of the sacred and admit our humanity. We allow ourselves to be fully vulnerable and ask for the support in transformation we all need. We do not fast by our own sheer will, but by seeking the ground of being that supports and nourishes us as we grow.

One of my favorite scripture passages is from the prophet Isaiah:

> *Now I am revealing new things to you, things*
> *hidden and unknown to you, created just now,*
> *this very moment. Of these things you have heard*
> *nothing until now. So that you cannot say, Oh yes, I*
> *knew this. (Isaiah 48:6–7)*

Ultimately, we fast so as to clear space within our minds and hearts and souls to await what holy newness is being revealed to us and to recognize it at work, as Isaiah says, "Created just now, this very moment." God is at work moment by moment, bringing new life to birth in places we did not expect. I love the second part of that passage, which reminds us that the cynical part of our minds, which wants to say that we've seen it all, that nothing can surprise us any longer, is too narrow to witness what is unfolding right now.

My hope is that this book will be an invitation for you to expand your concept of what fasting might mean for you and the gifts it has to offer, a way to witness those things hidden and unknown. Not just to stop eating chocolate, but to fast from things like "ego-grasping" or control, so that, in yielding yourself, a greater wisdom than your own is revealed.

The second part of each call to fast—the embrace—is also essential. We become aware of and fast from destructive patterns in our lives and direct our attention and energy toward what is life-giving, toward our true hunger and the feast. We let go of something depleting so we have more space to embrace what is life-giving and to nourish our true hunger.

And then perhaps from these Lenten fasts, we will arrive at Easter and realize those things from which we have fasted we no longer need to take back on again. We will experience a different kind of rising.

A Clean Heart

A longing for change echoes through the psalms as the ancient psalmist prays in supplication: "Create in me a clean heart, O God, and renew a right spirit within me" (Psalm 51:10). This longing is for all that distracts us to be purified, released, dissolved, transmuted. This is work done in the heart. The heart is a dominant metaphor throughout the Hebrew and Christian scriptures as well as other religious traditions. These traditions see the heart as the primary organ of our physical, emotional, and spiritual well-being. It is also the dwelling place of the divine presence. When St. Benedict begins his Rule, he invites us not to "think about" but to "listen carefully . . . with the ear of your heart."

The Hebrew Scriptures describe the heart as an interior place where we engage in an active relationship with the Divine. Theologian Norvene Vest describes it this way:

> For the early Hebrews, the heart involved not just
> activity but also receptivity. They viewed the heart as
> the inner seat of the human's whole being. As such,
> it was the organ of capacity for God's very self: It
> was the locus not only of choice and motive but also
> of one's fundamental orientation toward life. In the
> heart, we are formed and reformed into the person
> we most long to be.

The heart is not just active but also receptive. It is the deepest core of who we are and the organ of capacity for God's intimate presence to us. The heart is the place of meaning-making, where we discover how we are called to be in the world. When we fast from the things that distract our attention, we are collaborating with the sacred in creating a clean heart and renewing our spirit.

Much like the way spring cleaning can renew us and create more physical space around us for new life to enter, so too can fasting free us from patterns and habits that distract us or are harmful, creating more interior space for new life to emerge in our hearts.

The Spiritual Practice of Fasting

Fasting from food is one aspect of the asceticism to which the desert monastics devoted themselves. They saw asceticism essentially as about letting go of everything that keeps us from God to be on a journey toward authentic freedom. Desert ascetics kept their possessions to a minimum and practiced fasting as a way of attending to the body. The goal was never fasting to the point of harm to the body. That was condemned (although there were certainly monks who did end up starving themselves).

But fasting, as one of the stories from the desert elders shows us, was about a deeper attention:

> *Abba Daniel used to tell how when Abba Arsenius*
> *learned that all the varieties of fruit were ripe he*
> *would say, "Bring me some." He would taste very*
> *little of each, just once, giving thanks to God."*
> *(Arsenius 19)*

I appreciate this story as it is less about denial of food and the pleasure it brings and more about savoring the sweetness of nourishment in a way that is mindful and full of gratitude. It calls me to truly savor the food I do eat, to linger over it, to celebrate the gift of nourishment—and to taste and pay attention to whether that is enough.

I am aware that many people suffer from various kinds of disordered eating and talk about fasting can be triggering if you have struggled with eating too much or too little. I encourage you, first, to always take care of yourself. Speak with a medical doctor to help you determine a course of care for your body. This book offers many different ways to fast, so please know you are encouraged to apply this wisdom to other areas of your life.

Asceticism is always meant as a practice in service to freedom—when it becomes a competition or is oriented toward achievement or is a compulsion, it no longer serves its purpose and becomes destructive. It then can be another way we distract ourselves from the sacred presence in our midst. The kind of fasting explored in this book is not a second attempt at dieting when New Year's resolutions have failed, only to be picked up for Lent. That would be a distortion of the deeper meaning of this practice.

John Cassian said that our calling must have its origin in God rather than in compulsion. When the path leads us toward greater love, we can trust the source of it, rather than some other motive for fasting.

Desert monks like Cassian lived extraordinarily simply in a stone hut, sleeping on a reed mat, with a sheepskin for warmth, a lamp to see by, and a container for oil or water. Food and sleep were reduced to the very minimum needed to sustain oneself so they could be on watch for God, meaning they could focus their attention on the inner movements of the sacred in their hearts. They kept silence so they could hear the voice of the sacred more clearly.

I use the term "monk" to refer to both male and female monastics committed to a contemplative way of life. The root of the word is from the Greek *monachos*, which means single-hearted. A monk is one who cultivates a way of being that keeps their attention on the deeper dimension of life and how Spirit is moving. I believe any of us longing for a life of greater simplicity, silence, and slowness can call themselves a monk.

The desert ammas and abbas, as they were also called, never viewed fasting as something to be done for its own sake. When we fast from food, we are called to become keenly aware of our relationship to food and to pay attention to our own hungers. When we fast from the comforts of our lives, the invitation is to stretch ourselves and become present to what happens when we don't have our usual securities to rely upon. One meal a day was considered sufficient, and among other things, that commitment brings us into solidarity with those who are unable to afford adequate food.

Practicing this kind of letting go each day, whether it be regarding our own possessions, or consuming less, or giving more to those in need, or letting go of the hold our compulsive thoughts have on us, releasing expectations—all of these prepare us for the bigger moments of letting go.

Fasting is an invitation into authentic freedom, freedom from the things that weigh us down or keep us constricted. These might be material possessions, stories, or beliefs. Another way the desert monks fasted was setting words and conversation aside in order to create more internal space for transformative work. As Abba Isidore of Pelusia said,

> *To live without speaking is better than to speak*
> *without living. For the former who lives rightly*
> *does good even by his silence but the latter does no*
> *good even when he speaks. When words and life*
> *correspond to one another they are together the whole*
> *of philosophy. (Isidore of Pelusia 1)*

Abba Isidore's words speak to another kind of fasting, fasting from false speech or ideas that keep us from truly living, fasting from that which doesn't truly nourish us in spirit. We all hold onto old ideas about ourselves that keep us limited in what we believe we can do with our lives. We all fill our lives with words as a way to avoid what is really happening within us—whether we do that by our own words, repeating old stories, or turning up the radio or television to be saturated with the words of others.

I know for myself; I absolutely adore books. They are essential to my work and writing and I can easily justify the many bookcases in our home overflowing with volumes of great wisdom. The problem arises when I hear about a new book, and I reach to purchase it (so easy to do now in these online times). I have learned to check in with myself: Do I really need this? Am I avoiding deepening into my own wisdom by relying on the words of others? This is a delicate balance, because I deeply believe that books open up new worlds and I am firmly committed to my own ongoing growth.

But, like anything, books can also have a shadow side when they tempt us into believing we need more information about something to feel complete. Sometimes we buy more books as a surrogate for truly living what we believe those books to contain. The key is being fully present to ourselves and noticing where the hunger comes from in order to distinguish the direction of our desires.

The invitation from the desert elders here is, first and foremost, to fully live. That will mean different things to each of us, but we all have experienced something bringing us alive. And each of us has ways of avoiding that very aliveness. One story about the teaching of Abba Anthony records the following:

> *A brother renounced the world and gave his goods*
> *to the poor, but he kept back a little for his personal*
> *expenses. He went to see Abba Anthony. When he*
> *told him this, the old man said to him, "If you want*
> *to be a monk, go to the village, buy some meat, cover*

> *your naked body with it and come here like that."*
> *The brother did so, and the dogs and birds tore at*
> *his flesh. When he came back the old man asked him*
> *whether he had followed his advice. He showed him*
> *his wounded body, and Saint Anthony said, "Those*
> *who renounce the world but want to keep something*
> *for themselves are torn this way by the demons who*
> *make war on them." (Anthony 20)*

For me, this is one of the more difficult desert stories to read. Yet, the desert mothers and fathers offer us parables and imagery to shape our imaginations so that we are confronted with their message with a kind of fierceness. The stories are not meant to be taken as literal fact, but as symbolic truth and invitation. So, as I sink into silence and receive the words here, I discover a deeper layer for myself. This isn't so much about whether we give up all of our belongings to the poor, for certainly most of us would find that very hard to do. What I hear in this story is the call to be single-hearted in my commitments.

The root of the word monk is also *monos*, which means one or single. It is less about marital status as it is about the singularity and condition of one's heart. To live with singular focus means I commit to living my life with as much integrity as possible. Both the word "integrity" and the word "integrated" share the same root, *integritatem*, which means wholeness and soundness. To act with integrity means to always be moving toward wholeness rather than division within oneself.

Much of the suffering in my own life comes when I desire what feel like conflicting things. For many years I wrestled with my call as a teacher and a writer. My inner writer represented my more contemplative self, the part that could sit at the keyboard in silence for hours. My inner teacher represented more of my expressive self, the part that loves to engage with students and go on a journey of discovery in community. Teaching is also where I am more able to earn my living. This oversimplifies the tension, but my heart often felt divided between the two. If I had to teach too often to pay the bills, my contemplative prayer and writing were neglected. If I committed to solely writing, I would worry more about money and I missed the interaction and engagement with students.

I would love to tell you that I came up with a simple way to reconcile these. Really it has been a journey of seeing these both as integral to one another. Sometimes it is a season where I am called to focus more on writing, and sometimes to teaching, and sometimes I can live in a sweet place of balance between the two, moving back and forth. Even deeper than this is seeing that my calling at its root is about love and learning how to share my gifts in the world as a way to nurture that love. Anything I do that pulls me away from this focus causes internal division. If I don't care for my body well, my ability to express love through my work suffers. If I don't live by the principles that I teach and write about, my heart is divided and I am not able to offer the fullness of myself. Returning to the wisdom of the desert and seasons of fasting has helped remind me what *integration* means, what it can look like in my life.

Humility

This simple story from the desert's Abba Macarius brings us to the starting point of integration—humility:

> One day one of the young men asked him: "Abba, tell us about being a monk." And the wisest of monks replied: "Ah! I'm not a monk myself, but I have seen them." (St. Macarius)

Humility, as we'll see in this story from Amma Theodora, is also what is most needed in our inner struggles:

> (Amma Theodora) also said that neither asceticism, nor vigils nor any kind of suffering are able to save, only true humility can do that. There was an anchorite who was able to banish the demons; and he asked them, "What makes you go away? Is it fasting?" They replied, "We do not eat or drink." "Is it vigils?" They replied, "We do not sleep." "Is it separation from the world?" "We live in the deserts." "What power sends you away then?" They said, "Nothing can overcome us, but only humility." "Do you see how humility is victorious over demons?" (Theodora 6)

As a Benedictine Oblate I have made a commitment to live out monastic values and practices in my everyday life. Perhaps one of the most profound values for me is humility. Humility does not elicit much awe or admiration in our culture. It is a value that seems outdated or misunderstood in our world of self-empowerment and self-esteem boosting, negating much our culture holds so dear.

Some of the reservations about humility are legitimate, especially for those whose strengths have been diminished and marginalized, like communities of color and women. In these instances, abuse of humility can encourage passivity and low self-worth and can be used as a tool of oppression, imparting fear, guilt, or an abiding sense of failure, in an effort to remind people of their proper "place" and keeping them from rocking the boat or challenging institutions or those who hold power. There is also such a thing as false humility, when someone denies how good they are as a means to make themselves look even better.

However, healthy humility is a necessary practice for spiritual growth. The word is derived from *humus*, which means earth. Humility is at heart about being well-grounded and rooted. Humility is also about truth-telling and radical self-honesty. It is about celebrating the gifts we have been uniquely given in service of others, as well as recognizing our limitations and woundedness.

As creatures, we were formed in the image of God, which imbues us with profound dignity. The reality of our nature, too, is that we each carry a brokenness that affects how we deal with others. To deny this truth is to perpetuate the suffering that comes as a result of our limitations. Truth-filled living is the soul of humility. We are not divine, we are creatures with the spark of the divine. We are incomplete without God, the source of our own being, we are broken and wounded.

And it is humility that demands we acknowledge our source and our gifts, our dignity and wounds—as well as celebrate our blessings as a part of truth-telling. Humility teaches us to recognize that our gifts are not of our own making but are gifts we receive to be held in trust to give to our communities. Our gifts are not for ourselves alone.

Humility means setting aside our masks and brings us into a kind of nakedness where we allow ourselves to be seen without social convention, presenting ourselves in all of our vulnerability. Thomas Merton described this as the difference between the false self and true self. The fruit of humility is being at home with ourselves, our true selves, and being who God calls us to be because we have let go of living up to the expectations of others. You can understand, then, how essential humility is for the different kinds of fasting we'll explore.

Honoring our limits as creatures can be deeply liberating. We must have patience with the unfolding of our lives and the world. God's kingdom unfolds in God's own time. We discover that we are not solely responsible for saving the world. Acknowledging our limits can liberate us from our compulsions and frantic busyness and lead us toward recognizing our interdependence. Each of our gifts contributes to the whole. In his Rule, St. Benedict wrote about the ladder of humility, saying that as we ascend, so our capacity for love expands.

The practice of humility also leads us to a spirituality of radical newness and reversal. In John's gospel, the story of Jesus washing the disciples' feet gives us a vision of a new order and an image of encountering God in the most unexpected places. Humility is why we practice the spiritual life daily. We never fully arrive. We will always struggle in small and large ways. And that's where fasting companions us.

Practices like fasting, prayer, and solitude are not magic pills to end our inner struggles. If anything, they help to heighten our awareness of our demons—those things that, in the desert imagination, distract us from our true nature of love. By removing these demons that are distractions and ways of numbing ourselves, we can restore our focus on Love. We can return our singular focus to our true hunger.

The Seven Invitations of This Book

For each week of the Lenten season this book invites you to a different fast—from certain habits or patterns in your lives and the opportunity to embrace a complementary antidote, or life-giving practice that can support you in this holy work.

Starting with Ash Wednesday week, these opening days are a time to prepare yourselves and your hearts for this journey. When you embark on a pilgrimage there are certain things you need to do before you can take those first steps. I invite you to prepare the time and the space needed to enter these practices and to set an intention for Lent or, if you are using this book in a different season or for a retreat, then your intention for time or retreat.

For Week 1

You are invited to fast from multitasking and the destructive energy of inattentiveness. In our attempts to do many things, none are done well, and none as a result nourish us. The practice you'll look at instead will be a beholding of each thing, each person, each moment, as you respond to that hunger for presence.

For Week 2

You are invited to fast from anxiety and the endless torrent of thoughts that rise up in your mind, thoughts that paralyze you with fear of the future. Rather than scarcity, you'll enter into the radical trust in the abundance at the heart of things. You'll have the opportunity to listen to the hunger for contentment in the moment and to cultivate hope in the fullness of life.

For Week 3

You are invited to fast from speed and rushing through your life, causing you to miss the grace shimmering right here in this holy pause. Our culture worships productivity, and in its pursuit, many of us are depleted from exhaustion and hunger for slowness.

For Week 4

You are invited to fast from being strong and always trying to hold it all together, and instead embrace the profound grace that comes through your vulnerability and tenderness, as you allow a great softening within this season. We'll explore our hunger for the ability to reveal our wounded places and have them seen with love by another.

For Week 5

You are invited to fast from endless list-making and too many deadlines and enter into the quiet as you listen for what is ripening and unfolding, what is ready to be born. We hunger to release our own plans, our attempts to add more to our lists, adding to the overwhelm of everything in our lives, and behold what is actually emerging.

For Week 6

You are invited to fast from certainty and attempting to control the outcome of things so that you might grow in trust in the great mystery of life. While it may seem like we hunger for assurance and conviction about what will happen, when we can welcome in the beauty of the unknown, we can be nourished by new possibilities.

Contemplative Prayer Practices

Within each week's readings, you'll find a daily rhythm of practices you are invited to enter into. Each week begins with an introduction and reflection on the theme. Then there is a rhythm of daily suggestions for contemplative practice. While reading and understanding are important aspects of learning a new spiritual pathway, just as important is embodying these new understandings, practicing them, reflecting on them, pondering them in a spacious way that allows them to transform your heart.

The root of the word "contemplation" comes from the Latin word *templum*, which means a piece of ground or building consecrated for worship. When we contemplate, we consecrate an inner space in which to dwell for a while. When we move into a contemplative stance, we create a sanctuary within ourselves through which new consciousness can awaken and emerge, a consciousness needed to cocreate a more loving and just world. While society tells us we must always be doing and producing to bring forth anything of value, the invitation is to something counter-cultural and paradoxical: when we bring our heart, mind, and body fully present and slow ourselves down enough to truly listen to our hearts and the Divine Heart, we hear the creative responses that in our otherwise everyday rushings have no room to emerge.

When we practice contemplative prayer, we may meet moments of profound intimacy and connection to the underlying unity of all life. We may also have many moments of boredom and distraction. That is our human condition and the reason why we return to practice again and again. Our goal is not perfection but consistency. The great teacher of centering prayer Thomas Keating was told once by a woman that she struggled so much to greet silence and found herself distracted a thousand times. His response was to offer praise for the opportunity she was given to return to Divine Love a thousand times.

When we return to presence with compassion, we experience a profound grace. Each time our thoughts stray or we find ourselves unsettled, we are called to bring love to the whole of ourselves. Regular practice helps to cultivate within us an orientation to the Holy so that in the ordinary moments we become aware of the sacred presence. It can help sustain us through the challenging moments when God feels far away and we feel alone.

Through contemplative practice we also can move to a space beyond words, where our intuitive understanding comes to insights before we can articulate them. It is a heart-centered knowing that is receptive rather than grasping, intuitive rather than logical, and a slow ripening rather than a quick fix. In this inner spaciousness we begin to transform our wounded and broken places to remember our original wholeness. Slowly we become people who live in and respond to the world through love. Becoming people who live in the fullness of love is the deepest hunger of all.

Contemplative practice is at its heart a commitment to consciously enter into a deep sense of inner stillness where we release our life-denying patterns and ways of being in order to nourish ourselves and connect to the Sacred Source pulsating through our lives. It is a way of falling in love with the world and the divine presence that animates it. These practices take many forms across spiritual traditions. As you begin these fasts, it is worthwhile to experiment with different ways of praying to see which one feels the most life-giving in this season of your life and for the fast.

Theologian Tyler Sit, in his book *Staying Awake*, defines spiritual practice as "daily visits with God to build up a relationship and realign yourself with God's deep desires for the world." "Spiritual practices," he writes, "are disciplined truth-telling and truth-listening." As we consider how contemplation meets our journey of fasting, we might think of prayer as nurturing a friendship and intimacy with the divine presence. Lent is a time to augment this in a more disciplined way, meaning we show up even more steadily and open ourselves to the transformation that comes when we listen for the truth of our lives.

In connection to the fasts for this Lenten season I also invite you into a variety of contemplative practices, creating a holy rhythm for each week. Think of each of these ways of praying as a doorway into a different understanding, reflecting on, and embodying the particular call to fast for the week.

You will be invited to pray *lectio divina* with a text from the Christian Scriptures as a teaching story that can reveal new dimensions of what we are exploring. *Lectio*, or sacred reading, is an ancient practice and way of being led by Spirit to new insight.

Another ancient practice is breath prayer. It is a beautiful and simple way to rest into presence to this moment through words that are whispered on the inhale and exhale of each breath. In this way we can pray at all times.

In *visio divina* you are invited to pray with an image in a contemplative rhythm that is similar to *lectio divina*. I am very grateful to artist Kreg Yingst for creating beautiful and evocative block prints for each of the gospel passages suggested.

For those of you longing to connect to the desert men and women whose wisdom still shimmers across time, I offer a weekly meditation of one of their stories where you are invited into a personal encounter.

You will also be invited to go for a contemplative walk each week, which is a way to bring these teachings into the body and connect to the sacred in nature.

For those of you who prefer a more imaginative way of prayer and a creative way of entering into the Scripture text, I provide a weekly invitation into a practice that embodies the spirit of Ignatian prayer and Jewish *midrash*.

And finally, each week closes with a creative ritual to help you embody the practice more fully, along with a series of reflective questions that can act as seeds for new insight and discovery and a closing blessing to carry you forth with your new insight.

Day 1 of Each Week:
Overview of *Lectio Divina*

We'll begin the first day of each week with *lectio divina*, which I mentioned earlier, meaning sacred reading. It is an ancient practice of listening deeply to the voice of God shimmering in sacred texts. *Lectio* cultivates in us the ability to be fully present to the holy call that emerges from words. Words can illuminate our hearts; they contain seeds of invitation to cross a new threshold. Words ripen within us. We can receive a word and not realize its full impact for our lives for a long while, until one day that word opens in new ways and we suddenly see things differently.

The invitation of *lectio divina* is to cultivate a heart-centered intimacy with the sacred texts that is a different way of being with them than reading for learning and interpretive reasoning. Listening, savoring, and responding are different qualities being cultivated. And again, the purpose of this practice is that we gradually bring these qualities of being to the whole of our lives, where everything becomes a potential sacred text through which God can speak to us.

The practice of *lectio divina* is centered on some fundamental assumptions. First, the ancients believed that the Scriptures were like a love letter written to us by God. They are living and animated in an ongoing way by the Spirit. The texts speak to us in this unique moment of our lives, wherever we find ourselves. *Lectio divina* is not about acquiring head knowledge of Scripture, but about a profound encounter with the heart of God. We are called to nothing short of transformation.

Second, the Scripture texts and texts from other sacred wisdom traditions are an inexhaustible mystery that offer us an unending source of wisdom. No matter how much we strive to understand and integrate we will never reach the bottom of that mystery.

And third, God is already praying in us as we make ourselves available to join this unceasing prayer already happening in our hearts. God is the one who initiates the dialogue. Our practice is to make space to hear this prayer already at work within us through attention to memories, feelings, and images.

— HOW TO PRACTICE *LECTIO DIVINA* —

Preparation

A helpful place to begin is with your breath, slowing and deepening it and allowing it to bring you as fully present to this moment as possible.

As you settle into the rhythm of the breath, see if you can draw your awareness from your head down to your heart center. You might even place your hand on your heart to create a physical connection. Spend a few moments to simply rest here, feeling whatever the truth of your experience is in this moment, allowing it to have space. Then bring to your awareness what the mystics tell us—that the infinite compassion of God dwells within our hearts. Breathe in this infinite source of compassion and allow it to fill you in this moment.

First Movement—*Lectio*: Settling and Shimmering

Begin by finding a comfortable position where you can remain alert and yet also relax your body. If you find yourself distracted at any time, gently return to the rhythm of your breath as an anchor for your awareness. Allow yourself to settle into this moment and become fully present.

Read your selected Scripture passage or other sacred text once or twice through slowly and listen for a word or phrase that feels significant right now, and is capturing your attention even if you don't know why. Gently repeat this word to yourself in the silence.

Second Movement—*Meditatio*: Savoring and Stirring

Read the text again and then allow the word or phrase that caught your attention in the first movement to spark your imagination. Savor the word or phrase with all of your senses, notice what smells, sounds, tastes, sights, and feelings are evoked. Then listen for what images, feelings, and memories are stirring, welcoming them in, and then savor and rest into this experience.

Third Movement—*Oratio*: Summoning and Serving

Read the text a third time and then listen for an invitation rising up from your experience of prayer so far. Considering the word or phrase and what it has evoked for you in memory, image, or feeling, what is the invitation? This invitation may be a summons toward a new awareness or action.

Fourth Movement—*Contemplatio*: Slowing and Stilling

Move into a time for simply resting in an awareness of the sacred and allowing your heart to fill with gratitude for God's presence in this time of prayer. Slow your thoughts and reflections even further and sink into the experience of stillness. Rest in the presence of the Divine and allow yourself to simply be. Rest here for several minutes. Return to your breath if you find yourself distracted.

Closing

Gently connect with your breath again and slowly bring your awareness back to the room, moving from inner experience to outer experience. Give yourself some time of transition between these moments of contemplative depth and your everyday life. Consider taking a few minutes to journal about what you experienced in your prayer.

Here's an example of what this process looks like, if I were to pray with the passage I mentioned earlier from Isaiah:

> *Now I am revealing new things to you, things*
> *hidden and unknown to you, created just now,*
> *this very moment. Of these things you have heard*

> *nothing until now. So that you cannot say, Oh yes, I*
> *knew this. (Isaiah 48:6–7)*

To begin, I would read it through twice, listening for the word or phrase that shimmers. Now, in this reading, the line "things hidden and unknown to you" is calling to me. I might speak the words aloud to hear them. I let them echo for a moment in my heart.

A third time I read the text, letting that phrase unfold within me. I welcome in feelings of awe and reverence, memories of moments when the holy erupted in unexpected ways into my life, and an image of a dark womb space and the first tendril of new life emerging.

Then, a final time I read the text, this time listening for the invitation. Today, what I hear is to continue to trust deeply in divine mystery and to allow myself more space for rest, knowing Spirit is still at work weaving creation together. I bring the time to a close with silence and then journal about any insights that emerged.

Day 2 of Each Week:
Overview of Breath Prayer

Our breath is such an intimate companion. One that sustains us moment by moment even when we are entirely unaware. Yet when we bring our intention to it, it also becomes an ally for slowing down, for touching stillness. The ancient desert monks would pray with the breath as it helped them to follow St. Paul's invitation to "pray without ceasing." By repeating a short prayer on the inhale and exhale, breath prayer invites us to rest into the present moment. Breath prayers are meant to be gateways into here and now.

In the *Philokalia*, the great collection of Eastern Christian wisdom books, which also teaches about the early use of the Jesus Prayer, St. Hesychios the Priest writes: "let the name of Jesus adhere to your breath, and then you will know the blessings of stillness." I love this image of letting the prayer adhere to your breath. Rather than a forcing together of word and breath, imagine the words naturally being drawn to the breath like a magnet to metal or like bees to flowers. In this bringing together, the "blessings of stillness" wash over you.

Theologian Dr. Barbara Holmes describes breath as "the sustainer of life and also the vehicle for entry into the contemplative center. We take deep breaths to still our thoughts, center our being and connect to a wisdom that permeates the universe." Breathing sustains our bodies, but also brings us into communion with the sacred presence in all things.

Each week I will invite you into the practice of breath prayer. I offer a specific suggestion for the words to use; however, always feel free to adapt these as you desire. Maybe your prayer will emerge from the Scripture text you are invited to pray with in response to the theme. Maybe a prayer will spontaneously arise in your heart as you read about the theme and ponder how to live more fully into it.

The focus is not on saying each prayer correctly or perfectly each time, but to let the words open your heart to a deeper intention in daily living. We work on the words, but the words work on us as well. Eventually you might discover that you are not so much reciting the prayer as the prayer is reciting you, guiding you, opening your heart to a devotion to the sacred presence in this moment.

Another option is to let the word or phrase from your *lectio divina* practice become your breath prayer. I could take my phrase from the example above, and as I breathe in, I whisper "things hidden," and as I breathe out I say "and unknown to you." With each breath I allow the prayer to draw me more deeply into my heart to rest into the divine mystery. I can carry this as a prayer throughout my week and return to it in moments between appointments or times when I find myself waiting. Wherever we are, breath prayer becomes an anchor and a guide.

Day 3 of Each Week:
Overview of *Visio Divina*

The four movements of *lectio* we explored earlier are a sacred rhythm that cultivate our ability to experience God's presence in the world around us. One of the fundamental assumptions of *lectio divina* is that the divine presence is everywhere. We can apply the principles of sacred reading to praying visually with art.

I invite you into the practice of *visio divina* each week with the artwork by Kreg Yingst included in each chapter, which reflects a dimension of the Scripture text, or another piece of art that draws you. A simple way to find other art related to a particular Scripture passage is to put the name of the text in a search engine and then click the image finder and see what you discover. Praying visually is a different experience than praying with a text. For some it feels more natural and for some less so. Trust how you feel led to pray. See if you can approach the experience with an open heart and allow it to be a journey of discovery.

Settling and Shimmering

Close your eyes and prepare yourself for prayer by connecting to your body and breath, gently deepening the rhythm of your breath, bringing your awareness to your heart center. As you breathe in, imagine receiving the gift of vision, the sacred ability to see deeply below the surface of things. As you breathe out, imagine being able to allow your eyes to communicate love to others and to what you gaze upon. Allow a few moments to rest into this nourishing rhythm of preparing your eyes to behold what is before you.

Gently open your eyes and gaze upon the artwork softly with "eyes of the heart." This is a gentle receiving gaze, not a hard, penetrating stare. Move your eyes over the image, taking in all of the colors, shapes, and symbols. Bring a sense of curiosity to this image, exploring it with reverence, noticing all of its textures and features that come with seeing more closely.

As your eyes wander around the image in a brief visual pilgrimage, notice if there is someplace on the artwork that shimmers for you, somewhere that is stirring energy for you. Allow your eyes to rest gently there.

Savoring and Stirring

Be present to this place on the artwork that is calling for more attention. Begin to open your imagination to memories and other images that want to stir in you in response. Allow this place and these symbols or colors to unfold and open you to other connections. Notice if there are any feelings stirring within you and connect to your breath again, making room for whatever wants to move through you in this time.

Summoning and Serving

As the artwork moves your heart, begin to listen for how you are being invited in this moment of your life out of this time of prayer. Make space for your heart to be touched and for a longing to respond to God's call to move in you. Notice if the invitation wants to emerge, perhaps as an image or a symbol instead of in words. Ask how your life is becoming a work of art and how you are called to claim your place as an artist of this masterpiece. Where in your life are you called to bring more color, to bring more mystery, to explore what the artwork of your life wants you to discover.

Slowing and Stilling

Close your eyes if they are still open and release the images you have been gazing upon. Sink into stillness, slow your breath down, and rest in the grace of being for several minutes.

When you are ready to end your time of prayer, connect with your breath again and gently bring your awareness back to the room. Maintaining eyes of the heart, sometimes it can be helpful to gaze one more time following your prayer upon the image, taking it all in again, and seeing if you notice anything new. Then offer a moment of gratitude for the way this image has touched your heart.

As an example, consider looking at the opening image for Ash Wednesday week. Because this first week only begins on Wednesday, we won't engage all of the practices we have for the following weeks. But you can meditate with it as a way of practicing this visual prayer. Center yourself and let your gaze soften. Let your eyes take in the image as a whole and then make a journey around each element or symbol. When I gaze on it prayerfully, I see the mountains and cliffs, the trees, and the air and empty space surrounding the image. I notice the textures and lines, the contrasts. My eyes are drawn to that tree close to the center, reaching out from stone. I hold it in my heart for a moment and open to images of its roots extending into the solidity of mountain, its branches extending upward. I feel a sense of endurance and steadiness. I hear an invitation to be like the tree, remembering what earths me and what calls me to lift and reach. I close with silence and then some journaling. While the image that calls you may be different, trust the process and that which shimmers.

Day 4 of Each Week:
Overview of Meditations
with the Desert Elders

The desert mothers and fathers were people who fled from the cities in fourth-century Egypt, Syria, and Palestine, to live a more intentional life dedicated to the ongoing awareness of the divine. Their teachings were left behind in the form of short stories and sayings, much like koans in the Zen Buddhist tradition. The sayings are not always linear or logical but invitations to us to rest into paradox.

Thomas Merton was a big fan of the desert monks and suggests their wisdom is prescient for us today:

> *It would perhaps be too much to say that the world*
> *needs another movement such as that which drew*
> *these [monastics] into the deserts of Egypt and*
> *Palestine. Ours is certainly a time for solitaries and*
> *for hermits. But merely to reproduce the simplicity,*
> *austerity and prayer of these primitive souls is not a*
> *complete or satisfactory answer. We must transcend*
> *them, and transcend all those who, since their time,*
> *have gone beyond the limits which they set. We must*
> *liberate ourselves, in our own way, from involvement*
> *in a world that is plunging to disaster. But our*
> *world is different from theirs. Our involvement in it*
> *is more complete. Our danger is far more desperate.*
> *Our time, perhaps, is shorter than we think.*

Merton wrote these words in 1960, but they seem even more appropriate for our times now. Our involvement in the demands of this world, with its mindset of capitalism, valuing productivity, success, and staying strong above all else, is destroying us and the planet. The desert monks offer us a template for how to transcend the temptations in our midst and plunge ourselves into the beating heart of life. It is up to us to translate this into our own context.

The interior freedom that fasting can bring is at the heart of the desert journey. Fasting was one of the desert elders' core spiritual practices to help free their attachments to things and thoughts. They have much wisdom to offer us on our Lenten retreat.

Each week I will be offering one of the sayings of the desert mothers and fathers to pray with in particular. This is meant to be a doorway into meditation where you invite in the presence of one of these elders and listen for the wisdom they offer, as well as receive the gifts and blessings they give.

Reading through the description of the desert experience, you might then let your imagination wander or pray as you read, or you might even wish to record yourself leading the prayer and then listen to the prayer and relax into it.

Do not worry if your mind wanders. This is natural. Sometimes our daydreaming brings us to new insight about our lives and how God is calling to us in the midst of things. Sometimes we may become distracted by other things we need to do. When this happens, gently bring your awareness back to the meditation. If all you do is rest in the cave of your heart with the wisdom of the desert elders, that is enough.

During each meditation you will receive a particular gift as well. You are invited either to find a physical symbol of that gift to place on your altar or to carry it with you through your days as an imaginative talisman, a reminder of your pilgrimage through the desert.

Day 5 of Each Week:
Overview of Contemplative Walking

I also invite you into a practice of contemplative walking each week, if you are able-bodied, as a way to embody the themes we are exploring and see what you discover when you walk out in the world holding the intentions and prayers of this retreat. Often when we make a commitment to soul, synchronicities start to arise—through dreams, encounters with others, and daily events. This is also a way to grow in our intimacy with the natural world.

If you are unable to walk through the following steps for any reason, consider sitting by a window and letting your imagination take you on a pilgrimage through what you see, perhaps adapting elements of this contemplative practice to your unique situation, environment, or view. You can also make a pilgrimage of memory, if you have any memories of wandering in places you love. You can let your imagination take you through a scene and tend to what shimmers. Another option is to find a nature documentary online and turn the volume off and let your eyes take in the experience and notice what stirs in your heart. If sight is an issue, then listening to nature sounds can be another way to experience this, or being outside and engaging your senses of smell, hearing, and touch. Texture and fragrance are as much a vital part of our encounter with the world as vision is.

A contemplative walk is where your only walking focus is on being present to each moment's invitation as it unfolds, rather than setting out with a particular goal. There is nowhere to "get to." There are no steps to count, no minimum heart-rate to achieve.

Here's an overview of the general experience. First, I will offer specific ways of directing your attention in connection with the theme of the week.

You begin your walk by breathing deeply and centering yourself, bringing your awareness down to your heart center. Try to maintain a connection to your heart wisdom and to seeing throughout your walk. When you go out in the world for a walk, it could be in your backyard, just down your block, or in a nearby park. You can also do this in your imagination if walking isn't accessible to you for any reason.

If you would like to you can bring a camera with you— or the camera on your phone, that's fine. As you walk, stay present to the world as a sacred text. When we are on a thresh-old of prayer every moment has the potential to be a portal into how the Divine presence is speaking to us. This can be another way of engaging in *visio divina*. However, don't let the camera take you out of the present moment by thinking about the walk as a photographic opportunity, for posting the photos on your social media account in the future. Simply let the image be a portal to deeper seeing.

As you walk and see the world with the eyes of your heart, you will discover a way of seeing from an attitude of receptivity and openness, rather than focusing with the mind, which is often the place of grasping and planning.

When you walk, you are walking to notice and discover. You are walking to be a witness to the world in this moment, here and now.

As you begin walking, pay attention to things around you that shimmer, which means something that calls for your attention, invites you to spend some time with it. It might be a natural object like a tree or branch, it might be a sign in a shop window that catches your attention, or the way light is flooding the street. Stay open to all possibilities for how the world might speak to your heart. Stay with what shimmers and allow it to unfold in your heart, savoring your experience.

Make space within for images, feelings, and memories to stir. How does your body respond? What are you noticing happening inside in response to this experience? How does this shimmering moment meet you in this particular time of your life? How might you be called into a new awareness through this experience?

Explore with your camera how gazing at this shimmering moment through the lens supports you in seeing it more deeply. The practice of contemplative photography is to "receive images as gifts" rather than to "take photos." If you notice yourself grasping or overly thinking about taking or framing a photo, put the camera down. But if the lens is helping you to see this moment from different perspectives and deepening into it, then consider the camera a great companion and gift for this spiritual practice.

Once your walk, your contemplative time, feels complete, as you return home, release all of the words and images. Do not actively think about your task anymore, and slow down even more deeply. Allow yourself some time for silence and stillness. Breathe gratitude in and out. Simply notice your experience.

Day 6 of Each Week:
Imaginative Prayer

This form of imaginative prayer takes its inspiration from St. Ignatius of Loyola and also has roots in the Jewish practice of *midrash*.

Ignatius believed that our imagination, senses, and feelings were holy vessels and portals into understanding the sacred. He invites us to read a Scripture text prayerfully and then to imagine stepping into the story ourselves—seeing, hearing, tasting, smelling, and feeling what it is like to be in the scene.

He suggests that, in our imaginations, we have conversations with the characters to see what they might say to us—something known as a *colloquy*. This kind of prayer is about entering ourselves within the story, both body and soul, and seeing what we encounter. These words of the sacred texts are meant to be alive, and because they are archetypal, they can speak to human experience across time and to us, personally.

This practice differs from *lectio divina,* where we listen for a particular word and let that unfold within us, leading to insights and a sense of invitation. Ignatian prayer calls us to enter the story in a different way, seeing ourselves there within that context, in the landscape, interacting with the characters, both human and more-than-human.

Also helpful in contemplative imagination is considering the ancient Jewish tradition of *midrash*. Rabbis wrote *midrash* to help explain problems they encountered in the biblical texts, such as inconsistencies or missing voices. These stories formed around texts as an important part of the Jewish sacred literature.

Theologian Dr. Wilda Gafney describes the source of *midrash* as the sanctified imagination: "The sanctified imagination is the fertile creative space where the preacher-interpreter enters the text, particularly the spaces in the text, and fills them out with missing details: names, back stories, detailed descriptions of the scene and characters and so on." Our imagination is holy and can reveal truth to us.

In Judaism, Scripture is sometimes described as black fire on white fire, where black fire is the words on the page. And *midrash* illuminates the white fire, the spaces between the words that are written. Through *midrash* we explore the gaps in the story, the missing voices, the silences, the wondering that is sparked in the interaction between the text and all that surrounds it, the known and unknown.

When in the sixteenth century St. Ignatius of Loyola, a Spanish mystic and founder of the Jesuit order of priests, offered a way of praying the Scriptures through the imagination, it was clear that praying in this way bore a kinship to the ancient Jewish tradition of *midrash*. Now often referred to as Ignatian prayer of the imagination, we are invited into the cracks and spaces of the story to see what is revealed to us.

Both of these practices, *midrash* and Ignatian prayer, embrace the profound significance biblical stories can have for us personally when we allow ourselves to not just read at a distance but also enter into the stories with all of our senses attuned. Rather than just studying them or hearing the texts read to us from a lectern at church, these practices call us to dive into the story fully and see what we discover. These practices acknowledge the truths that can arise in our imaginative engagement around sacred texts.

Each week I will lead you through this process with our Scripture passage. You are invited to let this be both playful and profound. After the prayer is completed, you may wish to spend some time writing about your experience and perhaps create your own *midrash* text, where story and commentary and imagination all combine.

Day 7 of Each Week:
Overview of Rituals, Reflection Questions, and Closing Blessing

The purpose of ritual is to embody and enact our connection to the holy. It is a sequence of elements that include words, actions, movement, objects, or song. It is a way of intentionally entering into sacred space through symbolic action.

Lighting a candle can be a simple personal ritual when offered with the intention of focusing our attention on the sacred through the symbol of the flame. And attending a liturgy or worship service is among the more formal, communal rituals.

Elements of ritual include a series of actions that often have a set pattern that is repeated. The actions have symbolic meanings that point to something greater than the sum of its parts. And the ritual has no "useful" purpose as we tend to define "useful" from our task-oriented left-brained minds. Ritual is not performed with a specific outcome in mind, but with an openness to the unfolding gifts each moment offers. It is a way of honoring and giving reverence to the sacred nature of life.

Through their intentional nature, rituals remind us to call on the sacred presence here and now. They help to ground us in a relationship with Source so as to better navigate the uncertainty and anxieties of living in the world.

Each week you are invited to create a small ritual to help you embody the theme for the week through a sacred action.

These rituals of prayerful actions done with a sacred intention will help you cultivate a more intuitive way of knowing and listen for the language of mystery in your life. There will be a different suggestion each week, but always feel free to adapt as needed or follow your own intuition around which ritual may be a fitting practice.

Reflection Questions

As the week comes to a close, and following your creative ritual, I offer you a series of questions to reflect upon to help integrate your experiences and open to new insight and connections. These aren't summary questions like in an exam where you need to find the "right" answer. Instead, think of the questions as lanterns that, as Phil Cousineau writes, help to illuminate our lives: "Think of the ways that questions illuminate the world around us. Questions tune the soul. The purpose behind questions is to initiate the quest."

The questions are meant to set us deeper on our journeys. Allow the questions to have space within you so that if you find yourself rushing toward finding the answer, you instead might pause and notice that desire for a rush toward answers. Bring compassion for the desire. And then slowly let your grip on answers soften.

The poet Rainer Maria Rilke writes in his book *Letters to a Young Poet*:

> *I want to beg you, as much as I can, to be patient*
> *toward all that is unsolved in your heart, and to try*
> *to love the questions themselves like locked rooms*
> *and like books that are written in a very foreign*
> *tongue. Do not now seek the answers, which cannot*
> *be given to you because you would not be able to*
> *live them. And the point is, to live everything. Live*
> *the questions now. Perhaps you will then gradually,*

> *without noticing it, live along some distant day into*
> *the answer.*

These are questions for living into. Imagine draping them around you like a prayer shawl. Imagine they are birds flying across a wide horizon, drawing your gaze upward. Imagine they are openings to beauty and meaning that take time, like the unfolding of a rose's petals or the fermenting of a bottle of wine.

―――――― **CLOSING BLESSINGS** ――――――

Each week closes with a blessing I wrote for you. If you feel inspired, I encourage you to write your own versions. Blessings can offer hope and encouragement, steep us in gratitude, nurture our courage. They can help us to integrate our experience and feel witnessed. They help us cry out to God for the support we seek.

They bring us present to the grace of each moment. The word "blessing" comes from the Latin *benedicere*, which means to speak well of. Blessings help to remind us of the love and beauty of the Holy One in our lives and assist us in taking nothing for granted. Blessings act as maps to navigate our human experience, orienting us back to gratefulness and praise.

They sustain us in bringing reverence to all of life from the most ordinary of tasks to the great thresholds of our lives. They immerse us in the holy rhythms of the sacred, which are not of our making. In a world obsessed with the scarcity of time, blessings help us to expand each moment like a flower opening its petals on a sunny day. They invite us to breathe more deeply, enlarge our vision, and give honor to our experiences. Blessings help us to touch eternity here and now.

St. Benedict wrote in the Prologue to his Rule, "Let us get up then, at long last, for the Scriptures rouse us when they say: *It is high time for us to arise from sleep* (Rom.13:11). Let us open our eyes to the light that comes from God, and our ears to the voice from heaven that every day calls out this charge: *If you hear [God's] voice today, do not harden your hearts'* (Ps 94:8)." The image of awakening calls us to shake off the slumber that creates a veil between reality and our perception. And the act of blessing can help us to awaken and see more clearly. When we remember to bless, we consecrate life, whether we are in the kitchen, the office, in church, or standing in a forest.

Each one of these practices is an invitation and a way to bring the gifts of fasting near. They are meant to be guides and a place to begin and you are invited to make them your own. Adapt them. If you feel inspired in a different direction on a particular day, trust yourself and the sacred impulse toward prayer in whatever form it takes.

A Retreat in Everyday Life:
Preparing Space and Time

While being able to take time out of our lives to go to a retreat center or monastery for an extended period of prayer is a gift, it is also something that not everyone can do and has inherent privilege of time and opportunity within it. But all of us can create a retreat in our everyday life and enjoy its own gifts. By setting up a rhythm of daily practice—wherever we are, whatever situation we are in—we are nurturing life-giving habits and ways of being in the midst of our ordinary lives.

One of the understandings that Cyprian Consiglio, a Camaldolese monk and priest, offers us about prayer in *Prayer in the Cave of the Heart* is that this practice is to be performed anywhere.

> *All of this is mere verbiage without a commitment to daily practice. I have come to know that spirituality is eminently a practical science—it concerns what we do when we get up in the morning, how we spend our day, how we go to bed at night—and specifically how much time and energy we are willing to dedicate to the practice of prayer and meditation.*

One of the most important things we can do if we go on retreat—or bring a retreat to our daily life—is to prepare our heart space and our prayer space, and commit to practice.

Is there a place in your home where you can engage your regular practice? All you need is a comfortable chair and perhaps a place to keep a candle, a journal, and a pen. You may already have a designated spot where you like to pray and will continue to settle in there each day. You might need to create this space now and negotiate with family members or roommates if the space is shared with others. You can even designate your bed as your retreat place and create a restful nurturing environment that calls you back to prayer. Or it may be a place outdoors or on your front stoop.

Whatever space this may be, as we begin this journey, consider blessing this space. Simple words are all that is needed. You can write your own prayer or use these words as a suggestion or jumping off point:

> *Wilderness God, bless this sanctuary space that I*
> *offer to you, a meeting place where I can rest in*
> *your embrace each day, a vessel for transformation,*
> *a temple to journey inward. Sustain me in the*
> *coming days as I release that which does not nourish*
> *and guide me toward fulfilling my true hungers.*
> *I commit to returning here again and again, even*
> *when my attention wanders, I return to you always.*

I encourage you to make the prayer your own. Ask that your retreat space be a safe container for your prayer experience and that it hold you as you deepen into your practice these coming weeks. You might want to burn some incense as a way of purifying and consecrating the space, the way churches often do during liturgy to signify a dedication of the space to divine attention.

Then, if you haven't already, sit down with your calendar and write in time for your practice. I suggest twenty to thirty minutes each day to read through the daily invitations and enter into the practices suggested. You might want to have a slightly longer time at the end of each week for returning to any prayer practices that felt especially fruitful and to spend time integrating what you are discovering. Repetition of a particular prayer is not a rote rereciting, but an opportunity to delve even more deeply into its invitation to us. It is through these holy pauses and spaces for rest that transformation has room to enter in.

Reading the material is meant as a support to you, but the main work happens—as Father Cyprian writes—in the commitment to show up each day and let the process work within you. The act of reading these pages represents your commitment to nurturing an alternative way of being in the world and opening your heart to a more intimate relationship with God. The act of practicing these various forms of prayer is an act of trust in the transformational power of contemplation.

Always be gentle with yourself. Yes, there will be days when you miss your practice. Remember that St. Benedict counsels us to always be a beginner in the spiritual life. We are called to recommit ourselves again and again. The monastic commitment of conversion isn't about a one-time renewal, but a lifetime of discovery. Each time we drift away, we are invited to return with our whole hearts. Conversion means we resist cynicism and the belief that nothing new can happen within us or in the world. It means being open to holy surprise.

If in this coming season you have a day when you just don't feel like praying, whether because you are exhausted, depleted, feeling torn down by life, or simply uninspired, consider this reflection on the nature of prayer that writer Sophfronia Scott offers in her book *The Seeker and the Monk*, where she thinks she cannot pray and converses in imagination with Thomas Merton:

> *I asked myself this question: What if all my previous prayers—especially the specific practices in church or in my prayer spaces at home—were the equivalent of a large bird flapping its wings in preparation for flight? Then in times of trial, when I think I cannot pray, perhaps that's when I have somehow taken off. I'm supposed to glide—be present, trust the current of air, of spirit, to uphold me so I can do what is necessary in the crisis. . . . Instead of an absence of prayer, I am surrounded by prayer, effortless prayer.*

The days you are able to show up to the prayer practices, you are strengthening your muscles and capacity for flight. The days when it does not feel possible, I encourage you to at least show up to your prayer space for fifteen minutes, even if it is to sit in quiet prayer, resting and surrendering to the great current of divine love carrying you until you can take the initiative again.

What Is Your Intention?
What Is Your Deep Desire?

And we begin this time of retreat, where we first began: with intention. Allow some time to sit in your prayer space and listen. What is the deep desire of your heart for this season ahead? An intention is a commitment to direct our attention a certain way. It is never meant to be a rigid taskmaster. Often, we begin a spiritual practice, an approach to fasting, a retreat with one longing, and as the season or retreat begins to work on us, we discover a deeper desire hidden beneath the longing we stated, one which we weren't in touch with initially. An intention can be personal, but can also be global in nature if there is a situation in the world or your community you wish to pray with.

For any journey, spiritual or physical, it can be valuable to sit for a time in preparation. It is like booking a trip to go on a pilgrimage, spending time packing your bags, and then allowing some time to really tune into what is stirring in your heart. What are you longing for in your life right now? Is there a specific question you are holding? As you bring the questions to the start of the journey ahead, my hope is that the longings, the fasting, the invitations, and the practices will answer not only the intention but also the deeper hunger behind the question.

Once you have named your heart's desire you may want to write it in your journal and then light a candle, speaking your intention aloud. Let this be an act of consecration of the coming days and a symbol of your commitment to showing up to practice.

Let's begin our journey together into the wilderness of the heart.

Ash Wednesday Week

AN INVITATION TO
FAST FROM CONSUMING

EMBRACE SIMPLICITY

Ash Wednesday Week Reflection

IN ANCIENT TIMES, wise men and women fled out into the desert to find a place where they could be fully present to God and to their own inner struggles at work. They sought out radical silence, solitude, and continuous prayer. The desert became a place to enter into the refiner's fire and be stripped down to their holy essence. The desert was a threshold place where you emerged different from when you entered.

Ash Wednesday marks the starting point of the Lenten season. As it is midweek, our first "week" of Lent has only four days of practice, while the remaining six weeks will have seven days of practice each. This first exploration initiates the pilgrimage through Lent. It's a time to create space for your practice and to listen for your intention or deep desires of your heart.

If you participate in a liturgical service on Ash Wednesday, most likely you will be marked on the forehead with the sign of ashes, and the words "from dust you came and to dust you shall return" or similar words will echo through the sanctuary space again and again.

That Lent begins with a reminder of death can be daunting. In the monastic tradition, death is a friend and companion along the journey. St. Francis of Assisi referred to death as "sister" in his famous poem "The Canticle of Creation." And the desert monastics understood the necessity of that companionship—that reality—of our lives. St. Benedict writes in his Rule to "keep death daily before your eyes" (RB 4:47), and Amma Sarah, one of the desert mothers said, "I put my foot out to ascend the ladder, and I place death before my eyes before going up it" (Sarah 6).

The word for desert in Greek is *eremos*, which literally means "abandonment" and is the term from which we derive the word "hermit." The desert was a place of coming face to face with loneliness and death. Your very existence is threatened in the desert, which is why so many choose the desert to strip away distraction and focus on essentials—life, survival. The desert helps you face up to yourself and to your temptations in life that distract you from a wide-hearted focus on the presence of the sacred in the world.

Death of any kind is rarely a welcome experience. We resist death; we try to numb ourselves from life's inevitable stripping away of our "secure" frameworks. We spend so much energy and money on staying young. But when we turn to face death wide-eyed and fully present, when we feel the fullness of the grief it brings, we also slowly begin to discover the new life awaiting us.

Rather than a presence only at the end of our lives, death, as St. Francis wrote, can become a companion along each step, heightening our awareness of life's beauty and calling us toward living more fully. Living with Sister Death calls us to greater freedom and responsibility.

Alan Jones describes the desert relationship to death in this way: "Facing death gives our loving force, clarity, and focus . . . even our despair is to be given up and seen as the ego-grasping device that it really is. Despair about ourselves and our world is, perhaps, the ego's last and, therefore, greatest attachment."

If death can teach us to cherish our moments more deeply, it also helps us to let go of what burdens us—whether thoughts or actions or possessions.

At times when I became ill or when a loved one was dying, the essentials of my life became so clear. Love and friendship, kindness and compassion, these were the things that remained when all the rest dissipated in the moment that my attention became focused on life.

As I mentioned in the introduction, the desert elders held to different kinds of fasts, from food to possessions, in order to keep their distractions to a minimum. In this way they could focus themselves on their inner work and greater intimacy with the divine. These exterior practices of fasting were meant to clear the way to ultimately surrender their inner attachments, which also hindered their connection to the sacred, moment by moment.

In the Western world many of us live with easy access to an abundance of food. But much of it isn't truly nourishing for our bodies, and when disconnected from a community to share it with, it doesn't nourish our souls either. Many places are considered to be "food deserts," where fresh and nourishing food is not accessible at all. The USDA reported in 2017 that 19 million people in the USA live in low-income areas that are more than a mile from a food market in urban and suburban areas and more than ten miles away in rural areas. All that can be accessed is processed, fast food.

True feasting, the kind we do at certain times of the year like Christmas celebrations or other family gathering times, holds meaning and ties to fasting. If we feasted all the time, then these feasts would lose their value and significance. Similarly, the gift-giving we do at special times of year also has its worth when we live in a simpler way the rest of the time.

These first few days of Lent, I invite you to consider those physical things you could do without, as a way to give more focus on the less tangible things that hold importance, like relationships. From there, in the remainder of the season, we will focus on patterns and beliefs that we can fast from to bring us into deeper connection with the Holy One. As you begin, ask yourself, How does Sister Death invite you into what is most essential? You might also consider imagining yourself at the end of your life: What things do you most want to hold onto?

Daily Practices

ASH WEDNESDAY
DAY 1: *LECTIO DIVINA*

> *Then Jesus was led up by the Spirit into the*
> *wilderness to be tested by the devil. He fasted*
> *forty days and forty nights, and afterward he was*
> *famished. The tempter came and said to him, "If you*
> *are the Son of God, command these stones to become*
> *loaves of bread." But he answered, "It is written,*
>
> > *'One does not live by bread alone,*
> > *but by every word that comes from the mouth*
> > *of God.'"*
> >   Jesus in the Desert (Matthew 4:1–4)

AS YOU READ the text above, you are invited into the practice of *lectio divina* or sacred reading, a kind of meditative reading I outlined in the introduction. Even if you have read a Scripture text dozens of times before, this practice helps you meet the text as if it were new, as if it were being spoken into your life at this very moment in new ways. Which indeed it is.

This story of Jesus is a powerful message about the need for preparation for our work in the world and the role that fasting can play in the journey. Jesus became intimate with his physical hunger, but when challenged and tempted to satisfy it with food, he shares instead his truest hunger.

As you imaginatively spend time with this story, arrive to the desert with Jesus as if for the first time. Be in awe of the hunger for Spirit that lured him to the wilderness for a radical encounter with the divine in his life. Know the temptations he experiences as your own.

Scripture gives us many ways to practice fasting. And the practice of *lectio divina* helps us understand what we're called to. Allow fifteen to twenty minutes for this practice. Begin by slowing your breathing and connecting to your heart center. We are trying to "listen with the ear of your heart," as Benedict writes so wisely in his Rule for monks.

Read the text through twice, slowly, listening for a word or phrase that shimmers. Read it again and allow the word or phrase to unfold in your imagination, welcoming images, feelings, and memories.

Read the text a fourth time and listen for the invitation being offered to you in the midst of whatever life is bringing you.

Then rest into silence for a few minutes to simply savor the gift of being in the presence of the Holy One.

Spend a few minutes at the end journaling any insights you received or new awareness. How is this text inviting you to be present during the Lenten journey ahead?

ASH THURSDAY
DAY 2: BREATH PRAYER—I AM FROM DUST,
I RETURN TO DUST

BEFORE YOU BEGIN the prayer, please reread the overview of the practice of breath prayer included in the introduction to the book. It will give you a foundational understanding, especially if this is a practice new to you.

The gift of breath prayer is that we can do this anywhere. I suggest you try sitting for ten minutes in stillness to anchor this prayer into your heart and then return to it as you remember throughout the day. You might set a chime alarm three or four times during transitional moments such as morning, lunchtime, evening, and night when you could pause and pray this again.

Every breath we take is a reminder of our first breath and our last. With each inhale we invite in the gift of life that sustains us moment by moment, just as we did at our birth.
With each exhale we release and practice the great release that will one day be our final exhale.
Breath offers us the beautiful gift of holding this paradox: life and death are sisters.

Ash Wednesday and the start of Lent call us to bring ourselves intimately into communion with our mortality as a way to breathe more deeply into our lives again.

Your suggested breath prayer for this preparatory week is an invitation to rest into this dance of life and death we all hold within our bodies. At every moment something new is coming into existence. In each moment there is something dying and being released. Each day we awaken to the morning present to the day ahead. Each evening we give thanks for the gift of the day and prepare to release into sleep's surrender.

Breathe in: I am from dust

Breathe out: I return to dust

As you inhale, remember that you are dust. Dust of this beautiful Earth. You are fashioned from the minerals of bones, stone, and mountain, which in turn are fashioned from stardust.

Astrophysicist Karel Schrijver and his wife, Iris, medical doctor specializing in genetics, write in their book, *Living with the Stars: How the Human Body Is Connected to the Life Cycles of the Earth, the Planets, and the Stars*, about how our bodies are quite literally made of stardust: "Our bodies are made of the burned-out embers of stars that were released into the Galaxy in massive explosions long before gravity pulled them together to form the Earth. These remnants now comprise essentially all the material in our bodies."

They go on to write: "we are, indeed, stardust, in a very literal sense. Every object in the wider universe, everything around us, and everything we are, originated from stardust." This originating from dust means that we arise from the light of stars, which have in turn released their glow and materials into the universe.

When we die we return to dust, we become part of the great life cycle on Earth. Compost is essential for new life to arise and emerge. Dying and living are woven together into the fabric of the universe.

When we practice fasting, it can become a doorway to clarity and contemplation of our bodies in new ways. Fasting makes space for meditation.

ASH FRIDAY
DAY 3: MEDITATION WITH THE DESERT ELDERS

> *Abba Daniel used to say, "He lived with us many a*
> *long year and every year we used to take him only*
> *one basket of bread and when we went to find him*
> *the next year we would eat some of that bread."*
> *(Arsenius 17)*

THE DESERT MONKS were known for their practices of physical fasting as a way to gain clarity over their true hungers and to engage in radical simplicity. This story about Abba Arsenius above invites us to consider our relationship to food, our body's true hunger, and what is "enough." But it also calls us to consider other material things we consume in our lives and how we can reorient our relationship to them.

Take some time to slow down your breathing and come into full presence to yourself. Drop your awareness into the cave of your heart and rest there for a moment with the Source of Love who dwells within. Bring that compassion to yourself and anything you hold during this time of prayer.

Invite in the presence of Abba Arsenius. Allow a few moments to see how this desert monk appears to you, his clothing, his appearance, his presence.

Read through the story above twice, slowly, and reflect on the things in your life you consume, from food, to beauty and personal-care products, to new electronics, for example.

Do an honest inventory of your life and how you engage with things. Notice which ones seem to spark a compulsive relationship with, for example, over- or under-eating, over-buying, over-engaging with social media. Notice what arises under your heart's loving gaze.

Ask for the abba's support in how to disengage more mindfully. Listen for his wisdom about how to create more inner freedom from this outer spaciousness. See what guidance he has to offer. Make a commitment to fast from one thing during this season ahead as a way to become curious about your relationship to it.

Imagine that he blesses you with simplicity and openness. He extends his hands to you and offers the gift of a handmade empty clay bowl. Receive it in your open hands and spend a few moments pondering the inner spaciousness the bowl creates. Imagine the things that fill this bowl up that feel distracting or compulsive, and consciously empty the contents of the bowl into the hands of the divine.

Offer gratitude for the abba's presence and wisdom and know you can return to him at any time in the sanctuary of the heart. Bring your awareness back to the room you are in and allow some time to reflect on what you have experienced.

ASH SATURDAY
DAY 4: CREATIVE RITUAL—CREATE AN ALTAR

FOR THE SEASON of Lent, you are invited to create a simple altar space as a material marker for the season and your intention. Find a space in your home—it could be a windowsill or small table, the corner of a desk, or even a portable altar in a small box. Allow some time to ponder what symbols would help connect you to this season?

An altar is a space where we indicate our desire to show up each day to our prayer practice. It helps to embody our desires for this season and time of retreat in daily life. An altar is a liminal space, meaning it becomes a doorway between worlds. It reminds us of our holy longing to connect to the sacred in the midst of the ordinary.

You might include a candle to light each day as part of your prayer time. As purple is the liturgical color for Lent, you might include a cloth that marks the season as part of your space. If you have a bowl at home, consider placing it in your altar space as well to remind you to keep your heart open and free of distractions. Each time you feel filled by other things, return your gaze to the bowl and imagine letting those things go and keeping that space open.

See if there are any other symbols that would help remind you of your focus for this time. Perhaps a cross or a natural object or an icon would help to support you. Each week of Lent you will be invited onto a contemplative walk and you can pay attention to symbols and objects that present themselves in nature, asking to be included.

Don't let it be too complicated. And remember, you can always add to it as the weeks unfold.

Reflection Questions

What is the physical fast you choose for this sacred season?

What are the foods or objects that clutter up your attention and your heart?

When you imagine setting these aside for a time, what images come to fill that open space?

When you consider your mortality, some things naturally surface as important. What do you observe becoming essential in your life?

What true hunger do you sense emerging when you strip away the excess consumption?

CLOSING BLESSING

Holy Creator,

you formed us from the dust of the Earth

gathering up mud and dirt

in your warm hands, molding and shaping

and sending your spirit through us

until we came alive

and breathed and danced and loved.

These dusty origins began

with stars exploding miles away,

with aeons of light expanding and contracting

to arrive in this tender human form.

May we remember

our roots in Earth's rich soil

and heaven's luminous reach.

May we know ourselves

as radically and tenderly flesh

but also radiance of spirit

sustaining our every moment.

May Death become a sister

as our friend Saint Francis taught,

a wise one to help us to see

all that is essential in our lives.

May she help us to yield

thoughts, patterns, and ways of being

which distract us and exhaust us

and empower us to inhabit

the fullness of Love's call.

Strip us of regret

so when our physical end

does finally arrive, we can step across

that bright doorway with arms wide

and hearts open, ready to be gathered

back fully into your embrace.

Week 1

AN INVITATION TO FAST FROM MULTITASKING AND INATTENTION

EMBRACE FULL PRESENCE TO THE MOMENT

Week 1 Reflection

IT CAN BE so tempting to think that in our busy lives multitasking will somehow make us more efficient and productive. We bemoan not having more hours in the day, but in the hours we do have our attention is scattered, and we're always trying to keep up. We spread our gaze between so many demands that we may get many things done, even as we discover checking everything off the to-do list didn't leave us satisfied or nourished.

St. Benedict wisely wrote 1,500 years ago that we are called to always be beginners in the spiritual life. The landscape of the desert is often understood as a place of new beginnings; it is where Jesus began his ministry. In the desert, we are confronted with ourselves, naked and without defenses, called again and again to bring back all of our broken and denied parts into wholeness.

For the desert mothers and fathers, the monastic cell was a central concept in their spirituality. The outer cell is really a metaphor for the inner cell, a symbol of the deep soul-work we are called to, to become fully awake. It is the place where we come into full presence with ourselves and all of our inner voices, emotions, and challenges and are called to not abandon ourselves (our bodies, our cells) in the process through distraction or numbing. It is also the place where we encounter God deep in our own hearts.

Abba Moses wrote, "A brother came to Scetis to visit Abba Moses and asked him for a word. The old man said to him: 'Go sit in your cell, and your cell will teach you everything'" (Moses 6).

In his book *Listen to the Desert*, Gregory Mayers describes the cell this way:

> *Abba Moses' "cell" is a metaphor for the imprisoned*
> *self. If our appetite for the truth is strong enough*
> *to shore up our crumbling courage battered by the*
> *relentless onslaught of life's experiences, then we are*

> *rewarded by the emergence of the essence behind*
> *what is considered our self. . . . There is a final sense*
> *to the word "cell," meaning "the liberated self,"*
> *wherein life becomes transparent and obvious. . . .*
> *"Your cell" has no walls, neither physical ones of*
> *mortar or wood, nor walls of flesh and bone, nor*
> *psychological ones defining a separate, independent*
> *self.*

The interior cell of our hearts is that place of interior freedom. It is not a physical building, although we may have a room or small dwelling where we can pray and reflect, where that structure becomes a metaphor for the interior reality. I love Mayers's imagery here of how our practice of attention to the holy brings an emergence of our essence behind our masks and persona.

Distraction is seductive because it doesn't make demands on us. But ultimately this deeper hunger for what is true and holy within will call to us through the veil of our diversions. This is a lifelong journey, not something we achieve fully, but an ongoing unveiling and revealing of who we were created to be.

Abba Anthony wrote a similar message: "Just as fish die if they stay too long out of water, so the monks who loiter outside their cell or pass their time with men of the world lose the intensity of inner peace. So, like a fish going toward the sea, we must hurry to reach our cell, for fear that if we delay outside we shall lose our interior watchfulness" (Anthony 10). For the desert mothers and fathers, interior watchfulness was the entire focus of their lives and part of their devoting themselves to unceasing prayer and awareness of the sacred.

The desert mothers also had wisdom about the cell and the desire we may have to wander away. Amma Matrona wrote: "We carry ourselves wherever we go and we cannot escape temptation by mere flight."

Amma Theodora offers us a story:

> There was a monk, who, because of the great number
> of his temptations said, "I will go away from here."
> As he was putting on his sandals, he saw another
> man who was also putting on his sandals and this
> other monk said to him, "Is it on my account you are
> going away? Because I go before you wherever you
> are going." (Theodora 7)

We carry our "stuff"—our issues, our struggles, our compulsions—with us wherever we are. While our impulse may be to flee to a new place when something is not working out for us, the desert wisdom is to stay and become present to ourselves just as we are.

Another dimension of the "cell" is the prison-industrial complex in the United States. There are many for whom the cell is not a place of voluntary retreat. Some who spend their days in prison cells learn meditation as a way to become

internally free. This can also be a place of profound transformation, albeit in the midst of the horrors of having one's
external freedom seized. I think of author and spiritual director Therese Taylor-Stinson, who writes about the need for
internal freedom in our human journey as a continual process
of discovery. In her powerful book, *Walking the Way of Harriet
Tubman*, she writes, "It is both a quest for a deep emotional
freedom as we begin the journey to emancipation and an
ongoing struggle as we pull back the layers of enslavement
that we encounter along the way."

Connected to the cell as symbol for the interior life is
the cell as cultivation of patience. The Greek word is *hupomone*, which essentially means to stay with whatever is happening, and this is similar to the central Benedictine concept
of stability. On one level, stability calls monks to a lifetime
commitment with a particular community. On a deeper level,
the call is to not run away when things become challenging.
Stability demands that we stay with difficult experiences and
stay present to the discomfort they create in us.

The cell, it seems, is the complete antithesis of our
rushed attention, of trying to get as much done as possible,
all at the same time. When we are focusing on the ways we
try to accomplish too many things at once, we are never really
present for anything.

Instead, in our cell, we are called to full presence to our
inner life. We cultivate the inner witness and watch as our
thoughts scurry between different states, notice our internal

responses to things, and observe when our minds move to distraction as a way of avoiding engagement with life. The cell is the place where we grow in deep intimacy with our patterns and habits. When we become conscious of our methods of distraction, we can learn to bring ourselves always back to our experience. In this attentiveness to our inner world, we can then bring this kind of loving gaze to our outer tasks.

To behold means to hold something in your gaze. To behold is not to stare or glance; it is not a quick scan or an expectant look. We can't multitask and behold at the same time. Beholding has a slow and spacious quality to it. Your vision becomes softer as you make room to take in the whole of what you are seeing. There is a reflective and reverential quality to this kind of seeing. You release your expectations of what you think you will see and receive what is actually there, and in the process everything can shift. To behold is to meet the subject of your gaze with love.

Writer Cole Arthur Riley, in her beautiful book *This Here Flesh*, describes this kind of loving attentiveness to the world: "For me, most simply, contemplative spirituality is a fidelity to beholding the divine in all things. In the field, on the walk home, sitting under an oak tree that hugs my house. A sacred attention." Riley goes on to describe wonder as the heart of this presence to the world and what holds her faith together. "We have found ourselves too busy for beauty. We spin our bodies into chaos with the habits and expectations of the dominating culture, giving and doing and working. . . .

We live depleted of that rest which is the only reliable gateway to wonder." When we rush through life, we miss the moments that spark wonder. When we miss wonder, life can start to feel shallow and without meaning or beauty.

We are so used to using our capacity for vision to take in our surroundings quickly, to scan over things, to confirm what it is we are already thinking. Seeing in this other way takes time and patience. It is the view of the desert, the vista of the cell. We can't force the hidden dimension of the world to come forth; we can only create a receptive space in our hearts in which it can arrive.

As we enter the first full week of Lent and "enter the cell," I invite you to fast from distraction and multitasking so that you might embrace the practice of attention and behold-ing, creating space to see things differently. In this open space you create, you may discover a hunger to behold life as it is.

Daily Practices

DAY 1: *LECTIO DIVINA*

> *Now while Jesus was at Bethany in the house of*
> *Simon the leper, a woman came to him with an*
> *alabaster jar of very costly ointment, and she poured*
> *it on his head as he sat at the table.*
> Anointing at Bethany (Matthew 26:6–7)

THIS MAY BE my favorite gospel story. A woman comes to anoint Jesus with costly ointment. It is a lavish act. The disciples who witness this moment object to the waste this represents; they tell Jesus the jar of ointment could have been sold to feed the poor. But Jesus corrects them and praises the woman for what she has done.

There are only five narratives of women that appear in all four gospels in the Christian Testament, including this one. And each story gives us a sense of its significance to those who were trying to create a picture of who Jesus was and what he valued.

Jesus is practicing full attention to the gift of the moment. As we read this story as *lectio*, multiple times we discover Jesus recognizes the grace the woman offers to him and he honors her for it. He celebrates her extravagance. In the verses that follow where the disciples are critical of her perceived waste, Jesus responds differently, not choosing to value rules and practicality over generosity. Rather than his being caught up in distraction, Jesus is present to her and her act of love toward him.

Pray with this passage through *lectio divina*, listening first for a word or phrase, then letting it unfold in your imagination, and then listening for the invitation in your own life. How might you practice a fuller and deeper attention to each moment? How is Spirit inviting you into this embrace?

DAY 2: BREATH PRAYER—FULLY HERE, FULLY NOW

THERE ARE ALWAYS a hundred possible distractions at any given moment. Whether external ones like entertainment or mindless scrolling on our phones, or internal ones like planning and thinking ahead to the next thing, worrying about something that is going to happen, or replaying a conversation in your head.

Being fully present can be difficult. Consider how many times you have a conversation with someone, and you are truly present to what they are saying without anticipating what you will say. This gift of complete attention to another is a rare gift.

Our breath helps to anchor us in the present. It offers us a way to focus our often-distracted minds. It can help us release the nonessentials. Breath prayer was originally created as a practice to engage in perpetual prayer and awareness of God's presence.

Breathe in: Fully here
Breathe out: Fully now

With each inhale, remind yourself of where you are. Gaze around the room; notice the walls, windows, furniture, how the chair feels underneath your body.

With each exhale, remember this moment now. Imagine you are drawing your attention back to yourself. I sometimes think of my mind as an octopus with multiple tentacles all reaching out in different directions. With my breath I can help withdraw all those reaching arms back to my center and keep myself focused on this moment.

This is a continual practice. You will find yourself distracted again and again. This does not mean you are a failure; it means you need to keep practicing. Keep returning to your breath, keep allowing your breath to anchor you in this place, in this moment.

DAY 3: *VISIO DIVINA*

FAMILIARIZE YOURSELF WITH the overview of the spiritual practice *visio
divina* in the introduction as you begin
this day's mediation. I invite you to
pray with the block-print image by artist Kreg Yingst that opens this chapter.

Allow some time to soften your gaze and simply receive
the image. Let your eyes wander over it, taking in the textures, the symbols, the patterns. Trace the lines on Jesus's face.
Notice the arch of his neck forward. Follow the flow of the
oil pouring forth over his head and the drop of oil at the end
of his beard. Notice the ointment jar and its design. See the
hands holding it steady emerging from her dress and its lines.
Spend time in the white spaces between as well as the darkness
of Jesus's cloak.

See what shimmers forth for you from this image. Is
there a moment or detail that draws your gaze deeper? Something that stirs your heart? Or challenges you? It might be a
small detail or it might be the image as a whole. Rest for a
while with it, noticing body sensations, feelings, other images,
and memories which arise.

Then let those things that shimmer, those feelings or
memories begin to unfold in your imagination, making room
for how your prayer wants to move. Ask if there is a particular

invitation for you in the midst of these images and feelings? What are you called to pay more attention to?

Rest your eyes for a few moments in stillness, releasing all that has come and just breathing into the silence. Come to a place where you can surrender the need to do anything.

After a time return your eyes to the image one last time and see what you notice. Is there any new dimension to the invitation given to you? Any new insights? How does this image support you in the call to fast from mindlessness and embrace full presence? Allow some time to journal anything you noticed or discovered.

DAY 4: MEDITATION WITH THE DESERT ELDERS

> *Amma Syncletica said, "There are many who live in*
> *the mountains and behave as if they were in town,*
> *and they are wasting their time. It is possible to be a*
> *solitary in one's mind while living in a crowd, and*
> *it is possible for one who is a solitary to live in the*
> *crowd of his own thoughts." (Syncletica 19)*

EARLIER, IN THE opening to this chapter, we looked at how the desert elders each lived in a cave, hut, or single room called a cell. This was central to their journey, to retreat to solitude with the purpose of staying fully present to one's own experience. For them the cell was an outward reality but also a metaphor for the inner life. It is a symbol for the soul work we are each called to engage and the place of our intimate encounter with the Divine.

Amma Syncletica, one of the women who fled into the desert to seek this kind of radical communion with the sacred presence, teaches us that it is not the cell itself that brings inner peace. We might live in an urban center and imagine that if only we could escape to a monastery or a quiet place by the sea, then we could become present to our lives. But her wisdom reminds us we can bring presence and focus in the midst of a crowd and we can also sit in a silent place and be overwhelmed by thoughts and distractions.

Allow a few moments to center and breathe deeply, drawing your awareness back to yourself. Rest in the presence of the Beloved who dwells in the cave of your heart, that interior cell where you are called to simply be.

Invite in the presence of Amma Syncletica to be with you. Notice how she appears to you. Read through her words above twice, slowly. Share with her the moments you have tried to meditate in a quiet place, only to have your inner noise overwhelm you. Similarly reflect on a time when you were in the height of busyness, but something brought you to pause and full presence to the moment. It may have been the way the light was shining or the look of love in someone's face. Listen for her wisdom in response.

Ask the amma for support and guidance in how to be more present to yourself and to your life. Share what most distracts you, whether replaying conversations in the past, planning for the future, worries, or other things that keep your attention from being fully here.

Imagine that Amma Syncletica is blessing you with strength and focus. Notice how this feels in your body. She extends her hands out to you and gifts you with a small beeswax candle. She lights it and invites you to allow the flame to call you back here and now. Because this is an inner flame you can carry it wherever you go.

Offer gratitude for the amma's presence, wisdom, and blessing, and remember you can return to be with her at any time.

Return your awareness gently back to the room you are in and allow some time to reflect on your experience.

DAY 5: CONTEMPLATIVE WALK

AS YOU PREPARE for your contemplative walk, first allow a few minutes to center in stillness. Let your awareness drop into your heart. Then, as you take the first steps of your walk, bring yourself as fully to the present moment as you can. With each step, engage the world through your senses of sight, smell, touch, sound, taste, and intuition. When you notice your awareness wandering, gently bring it back to here and now. Keep returning to your breath as an anchor.

As you walk through the world, be present to how nature is unfolding before you moment by moment. Pay attention to any signs or symbols that support you in the practice of paying attention.

What are the sights, sounds, smells, tastes, and textures shimmering for you? What does your intuition tell you about what is being revealed or offered?

If you bring your camera, stay open to receiving images that speak to you of presence. How does nature call your attention back again and again?

When you return from your walk, allow some time in silence and sit and gaze on the images you received (whether in your imagination or on your camera) with an open and curious heart. In what ways is your heart's deeper hunger for presence revealed?

DAY 6: IMAGINATIVE PRAYER

> *Now while Jesus was at Bethany in the house of*
> *Simon the leper, a woman came to him with an*
> *alabaster jar of very costly ointment, and she poured*
> *it on his head as he sat at the table.*
>
> *Anointing at Bethany (Matthew 26:6–7)*

WE RETURN TO the Scripture text once again, this time to enter the story in a new way.

Begin much in the way you would for a practice of *lectio divina*. Center yourself with some deep breaths, move your attention inward, begin settling into stillness.

Then read the text through slowly. Imagine that you are experiencing the story right now; it is not some distant mythical or historical account, but a story meant to become alive for you.

Let yourself enter the scene with all of your senses engaged. What do you see, taste, smell, hear, and feel? Allow some time for these to each reveal themselves.

Let yourself enter into each of the characters in the story. Imagine you are the woman pouring the sacred oil over Jesus to anoint him. What are you thinking and feeling? Imagine that you are Jesus, receiving this lavish gift. Imagine that you are the others in the room, judging what is happening as an extravagant waste. Enter into the voice of the jar, the oil itself, or whichever opening seems to invite you to step inside.

The important thing in this practice is not to let yourself get caught up in theological interpretation. For a moment, set aside your preconceived ideas of this story and other potential distractions of being present to the story itself and your present moment experience of it.

Let yourself meet the story as if for the first time and begin an encounter with it. Enter into it and see it in your imagination. What do you discover from this new vantage point?

Have a conversation with Jesus and the woman about each of their experiences and longings. How do they feel about this moment of intimate and holy connection? What are their hopes and fears? Do they have any wisdom for you as you begin your own great journey into the season of Lent? Or maybe you have a conversation with those who sit in the room and judge what is happening. What are the questions that arise for you from the text? You may find other invitations and engagements, but these are some suggestions.

To pray with the imagination and enter the story and to write *midrash* doesn't require special skill. The practice of *midrash* is essentially looking for the spaces in the story that spark your curiosity. Whose stories are not told here that you can bring voice to? What are you wondering about that isn't said? When we engage creative expression as a process, we let go of the fear of what the end product will look like and let ourselves yield to what the process reveals to us. Be attentive to your own experience as you move through, where do you encounter ease and where is the resistance? Just notice these with compassion and curiosity.

The most important part of this process is to pay attention to the moment in the story that stirs the most curiosity or energy for you. It might be the place of your greatest resistance, the place in the story that feels the most difficult. Stay with that energy. Where do the questions emerge?

Feel free to write in prose or poetry form. However the words emerge is perfect.

This kind of writing is a process of diving deep within and seeing what you discover. Let the process itself surprise you and take you places you didn't expect. Follow the thread of what is unfolding as you explore and seek wisdom.

Sometimes writing with a limited amount of time can be helpful. Consider setting a timer for ten or fifteen minutes, read the passage, and then see where your imagination takes you without judgment or without trying to force things in a particular direction. Time limits can be very helpful in bypassing our analytical minds that want to spend hours finding the perfect story and writing it in the perfect form with the perfect words. This process of writing in response is not about perfection or product, but discovery and encounter. When we write in a limited time-frame it can help us drop down below the inner critic and our own censorship just long enough to access something from the heart.

Set the timer and write. It might be the thoughts and desires of a single character of their experience in the moment.

It might be a journey of remembering or anticipation. Often dialogue, either between you and a character, or between the characters themselves can be a place for rich exploration. Or perhaps your story is just a description of the sensual richness of this encounter as you have encountered it in your imagination. You could also express this through expressive drawing, using colors and shapes to put to paper what you experienced.

DAY 7: CREATIVE RITUAL FOR THE SENSES

RETURN TO YOUR Lenten altar and expand it by adding symbols for the six senses. Our senses help to ground us in the here and now. They lure us into the present moment. You are building on the initial altar you created last week.

This time, include an item for each sense. For vision, you might choose an icon or other piece of sacred art or a photograph of a place you love. For sound, some sacred music loaded onto your smartphone or a bell or chime of some kind. For scent, some essential oil or a bouquet of fragrant fresh flowers. For taste, you might include a piece of dark chocolate or some nuts. For texture, a lovely soft prayer shawl or some lotion or other kind of oil to massage into your hands. For your sixth sense, your journal and pen to record insights and intuitions, or some drawing materials.

Make a practice today of sitting with each of these sensory reminders and offer gratitude for the way your senses help you to connect to the divine presence. Linger with each sense experience and bless this connection to the divine presence.

In coming days, as you return to your altar space you can let it remind you of your commitment from this week.

Reflection Questions

What would it be like to allow the one task at hand to have your full awareness?

What touchstones could you engage to help you remember to come back to the present moment? A chime on your phone? A stone in your pocket?

When in your own life were you met with lavish abundance the way Jesus was with the woman who anointed him with oil? How might you meet others in this way?

What kind of boundaries on certain activities and distractions might you need to set in your life to give yourself the gift of presence?

When you look at patterns of overdoing and overcommitment, what do you discover beneath those? What are they helping to distract you from?

When you consider fasting from multitasking and giving yourself over to each moment as it arises, what is the true hunger you discover?

—————— **CLOSING BLESSING** ——————

Holy Presence,

guide our gaze back to here and now

and reveal to us that you are with us always.

Awaken us to see each shimmering moment,

each loving gesture, each face full of yearning,

and the ways you dance through Creation.

Sustain us in releasing our need to distract

ourselves with things which do not nourish,

or numb us to the aliveness that is possible.

Help us to savor this world

through the gift of our senses,

so that each day we look for beauty,

we listen for the music of the world,

we relish our meals,

we inhale the fragrance of flowers

we feel the embrace of life.

When our attention wanders

to that which depletes us,

gently direct us again to your sacred banquet.

Week 2

AN INVITATION TO
FAST FROM SCARCITY ANXIETY

EMBRACE RADICAL
TRUST IN ABUNDANCE

Week 2 Reflection

AT THE START of each new year, I have a practice of choosing a word to guide me into a new season of life, inspired by the desert mothers and fathers who, when they sought out a wisdom guide, would ask the guide: "Give me a word." This "word" was meant to be a word, phrase, or insight that the monks could chew on over several weeks, months, or even years.

The first year I did this, my word was "surplus." It is a word that had been working on me for some time. A few summers prior, I was pondering how to make the work I love more sustainable both energetically and financially. Even with work that arises out of passion, we bump up against our limits of what we can give and how much renewal we need. I also have an autoimmune illness that amplifies my need to be discerning about time, rest, and sustainability.

As a contemplative and a strong introvert, my needs for quiet times are high and I am grateful for the seasonal rhythms of the work we do that allow for extended times of restoration. My husband and I generally take summers off from teaching to have time to write and dream into future programs. But there is, of course, always the anxiety around money and being able to earn enough to live.

Then a few summers ago my pondering shifted to consider something even more generous than merely sustainable: *surplus*. I was not just thinking about how to have enough energy and resources to meet the needs of the flourishing community I steward, but to have more than enough, a surplus, an excess of reserves.

My word was inspired by a quote by Jungian analyst Robert Johnson in his book *The Fisher King and the Handless Maiden*. The "Handless Maiden" story is one of my favorite fairy tales, which I have returned to again and again over the years because of its power for me. Johnson refers to the part of the story where the maiden goes off to the forest for seven years to find healing:

> *Nothing happens, which is enough to frighten any modern person. But that kind of nothingness is the*

> *accumulation or storing of healing energy . . . to*
> *have a store of energy accumulated is to have power*
> *in back of one. We live with our psychic energy in*
> *modern times much as we do with our money—*
> *mortgaged into the next decade. Most modern people*
> *are exhausted nearly all the time and never catch up*
> *to an equilibrium of energy, let alone have a store*
> *of energy behind them. With no energy in store, one*
> *cannot meet any new opportunity.*

What makes contemplative life so counter-cultural is the active resistance against living a life of busyness and exhaustion, of not making that a badge of pride, of having an abundance of time to ponder and live life more slowly and attentively. The ability to embrace a slower life is something out of reach for many who have to work multiple jobs to make ends meet or are single parents. Tricia Hersey, the powerful voice behind the Nap Ministry, writes in her book *Rest Is Resistance* that the "desperate and valid question of 'How can I rest, if I have to pay bills?' is the beating heart of this work." She goes on to proclaim rest as our divine birthright, and those for whom rest seems especially elusive are commissioned with the necessary task of resisting the endless grind of our culture. This is the call we all must respond to and to find ways to support one another in claiming this essential gift. These may be in the smallest and simplest of ways, such as closing your eyes for ten minutes and allowing yourself a moment to daydream or a short nap in the middle of the day. However we claim this space of rest, we can be assured that we are living into the abundance that exists and rejecting the false and brutalizing system of exhaustion we live under. Hersey goes on to write: "Rest disrupts and makes space for intervention, imagination, and restoration. Rest is an imagination too because it makes space to simply be."

We are surrounded by the reality of scarcity when those with means exploit the labor of others, as well as the continual messages of scarcity, so our anxiety gets fueled. One of the most profound practices to resist this kind of anxiety, to fast from its hold on me, is the practice of Sabbath. Walter Brueggemann, in his wonderful book *Sabbath as Resistance*, writes that the practice of Sabbath emerges from the Exodus story, where the Israelites are freed from the relentless labor and productivity of the pharaoh system in which the people are enslaved and full of the anxiety that deprivation brings.

Yahweh enters in and liberates them from this exhaustion, commanding that they take rest each week. Today, we essentially live in this self-made, insatiable, oppressive pharaoh system which keeps so many deprived of what they need to thrive. We are not literally enslaved the way the Israelites were, but we are symbolically enslaved to a system that does not care for our well-being. So weary are we, so burdened by consumer debt, working long hours with very little time off.

So many take pride in wearing the badge of "busy." So many have no choice but to stretch themselves thin to the very edges of their resources and capacity.

When we practice Sabbath, we are making a visible statement that our lives are not defined by this perpetual anxiety. At the heart of this relationship is a God who celebrates the gift of rest and abundance. But, Brueggemann says, we are so beholden to "accomplishing and achieving and possessing" that we refuse the gift of simply *being* given to us.

The Israelites, and we ourselves, must leave Egypt and our enslavement to be able to dance and sing in freedom the way Miriam did with her timbrel after crossing the Red Sea. Dance is a celebratory act: not "productive" but restorative. When we don't allow ourselves the gift of Sabbath rest, we deny the foundational joy that is our birthright as children of God. To dance in freedom is a prophetic act.

We are called to regularly cease, to trust the world will continue on without us, and to know this embodiment of grace and gift is revolutionary. Nothing else needs to be done. We fool ourselves so easily into thinking that, if we only work hard enough, we will earn our freedom. But the practice of freedom comes now, in the midst of the demands of the world.

Thomas Merton wrote in *Conjectures of a Guilty Bystander*: "Here is an unspeakable secret: paradise is all around us and we do not understand." This is a thoroughly monastic vision, to recognize that paradise or heaven is not some reality after we die, but a living presence now. Capitalism tells us the opposite, that we can buy paradise if we only work hard enough. When Sophfronia Scott read the words of Merton, she wrote: "I felt something open up in my whole being. It felt immense and small at the same time because it felt like one word: *Yes. Yes*, I thought. That's exactly it." This experience of divine abundance can make us feel both immense—connected to this lavish extravagance—and small, meaning human and limited in our capacity to fully understand.

Visual artist and theologian Makoto Fujimura asks, "What if what is central to God's reality is not the mechanistic, utilitarian survival of the species, but the exuberant abundance of Creation and New Creation?" When we yield to this experience and awareness of generosity and abundance, we are sustained in ways we can't summon from our own will.

In the coming days, as part of your Lenten practice, I invite you to fast from anxiety and the endless torrent of thoughts that rise up in your mind to paralyze you with fear of the future. As human beings, it is natural for us to feel anxious at times. But we can also choose to nourish ourselves with the antidote for anxiety and allow ourselves some freedom from the worry for a while. The more we practice this, the more we start to trust this possibility.

Reclaim the Sabbath, making a commitment to rest and to lay aside work and worry. Give yourself the gift of moments that are truly restorative—some time spent in silence, a beautiful meal shared with a friend, a long walk in a beautiful place, a nap. Sabbath-keeping is an embodiment of our faith that there is something deeper at work in the world than the machinations of the power structures. It is a way for us to embody this profound trust and enter into the radical abundance at the heart of things.

Daily Practices

DAY 1: *LECTIO DIVINA*

> *[Jesus] sat down opposite the treasury and watched*
> *the crowd putting money into the treasury. Many*
> *rich people put in large sums. A poor widow came*
> *and put in two small copper coins, which are worth*
> *a penny. Then he called his disciples and said to*
> *them, "Truly I tell you; this poor widow has put*
> *in more than all those who are contributing to the*
> *treasury. For all of them have contributed out of*
> *their abundance; but she out of her poverty has put*
> *in everything she had, all she had to live on."*
>
> The Widow's Gift (Mark 12:41–44)

SO MANY STORIES in the Christian gospels offer images that reverse our expectations of how the world should work given the cultural patterns we live in. Western culture magnifies wealth and idolizes the accumulation of goods and resources as a sign of success. In the gospel story, Jesus shows us the opposite. The widow in her poverty who has given two copper coins is more generous than all those who hoard their wealth and give a fraction of it.

It can be hard to trust in this abundance in a world that tells us everything is scarce, and we have to compete with one another or be left wanting. We live in a world where the rich get exponentially wealthier and those who are poor continue to struggle more and more to make ends meet.

This is not a prosperity gospel message where Jesus wants those of us who are poor or struggling to give away all of our funds in the hopes of some bigger financial payoff. But it *is* an invitation to the practice of generosity, which is its own form of abundance. To love freely, to give of one's time lavishly, to practice compassion without bounds. We are called to do this for ourselves as well as for others.

Read the passage in a slow, prayerful way, listening for a word or phrase, then allow that to expand into images, memories, and feelings. Finally, listen for the invitation being whispered to you this day. Let the images invite you into a new way of moving through the world, governed by surplus instead of scarcity.

DAY 2: BREATH PRAYER—TRUSTING IN DIVINE ABUNDANCE

BREATH CAN BE a wonderful ally in cultivating a deeper sense of trust in life and a sense of the abundance at the heart of the world. The simple act of slow, deep breathing helps to calm my nervous system, which reduces the anxiety I can often feel creep in around life's responsibilities. For a few minutes in the day, my breath becomes a sanctuary where I can feel the truth of Life sustaining me moment by moment. I can root myself into Love's abundance. I can practice trust in something greater than me that holds me in loving care. These can become Sabbath moments when we claim our freedom from the tyranny of doing and rest into the gift of being.

Breathe in: Trusting
Breathe out: In divine abundance

As you inhale, feel your lungs and diaphragm fill with life-giving oxygen and whisper "Trust." As you exhale, feel your body loosen and soften, perhaps the edges of anxious thoughts wither slightly as you release into the possibility of divine abundance as a gracious reality.

This deepening into trust is as much a physical reality as it is emotional or spiritual. When our bodies hold heightened tension and anxiety, it is very challenging for us to feel any ease or trust in our lives. Breath helps us to soften into this possibility. It is a practice I return to each day, tracking where my body feels tight and resting compassionately into those places with the softening power of the breath.

DAY 3: *VISIO DIVINA*

I INVITE YOU to pray with the block print image by artist Kreg Yingst that opens this chapter. Allow a few moments to center yourself and soften your gaze.

Let your eyes wander around the image, taking in the various figures, the towering men with their bags of money, their black garments, the widow and her clothing, her open hands with just a single copper coin in each, the whole of her offering. Notice the white space surrounding them all.

Find a place that shimmers or calls to you in some way and allow your eyes to rest there. Breathe with the image, noticing how it shifts with each inhale and exhale. Welcome in other images, feelings, and memories as the initial seed of the image widens in your heart.

Ask if there is an invitation for you here to contemplate, a new awareness or action. Rest with whatever might be showing itself to you.

If you don't sense an invitation, you do not need to make something happen; simply rest with the gift of this time.

Allow a few moments of silence at the end, perhaps closing your eyes for a while to release words and images.

When you open your eyes again, take in the initial image as a whole and see if you notice anything new. How does this image support you in your call to fast from fear of scarcity and embrace abundance? Spend some time with your journal writing anything you noticed or discovered.

DAY 4: MEDITATION WITH THE DESERT ELDERS

> *(Abba Poemen) said, "Do not give your heart to that which does not satisfy your heart." (Poemen 80)*

READ ABBA POEMEN'S saying through a few times, letting it become a mantra. *Do not give my heart to that which does not satisfy my heart.*

On one level it seems fairly obvious that we should only give to ourselves that which nourishes and satisfies. Yet how often do we make choices each day that draw us away from what is most vibrant and alive? Maybe it is scrolling repeatedly and endlessly on your phone in any quiet moments you have. Maybe it is eating things too quickly on the go. Maybe it is one of a number of other distractions we use to avoid our anxiety.

I know when I sit in meditation first thing in the morning it lifts my heart and soothes my spirit. I become grounded in Love's presence and then the challenges of the day become easier to respond to. What satisfies the heart is what helps us to rest into a sense of "enough" in this moment. It follows from the presence we explored in Week 1.

Today, spend a few minutes quieting your mind and resting your body. Gather your awareness back to yourself, letting it drop down into your heart. Rest for a moment with the holy flame within you.

Invite in the presence of Abba Poemen, this wise desert father. Welcome him to be with you for a little while. Listen as he repeats this saying to you like gentle waves of an ocean lapping the shore. Let the words sink more and more deeply into your being.

Reflect on the things you give your heart to that are not satisfying. Recall the last several days and notice what patterns you have that are depleting. Ask Abba Poemen to hold these for you and to help transform them.

Reflect on what does satisfy your heart, as you respond to the question: What nourishes and renews it? Share these with him as well and ask for his blessing as you welcome these into your life as gift. Listen for any wisdom he has to offer. He offers you a gift, a pomegranate, which he breaks in half with his hands and the red juice runs down over his arms. You take the sweet fruit and put some seeds in your mouth, letting the juiciness remind you of the gracious abundance of life. Savor its sweetness. Sit together for a while eating in the silence.

Gently return to the room you are in and allow some time for reflection.

DAY 5: CONTEMPLATIVE WALK

ON YOUR CONTEMPLATIVE walk this week, what would it look like to walk with trust as a companion? As you walk in the world, breathing slowly, paying attention to the signs and symbols around you, what does nature reveal about trust and divine abundance?

Walking is another act that for me can cultivate trust in the world as I witness nature unfolding around me; I see how the rhythms of rise and fall, fullness and emptiness are embedded into creation's cycles. Flowering and fruitfulness always return after a season of release, surrender, and fallowness.

This is a powerful practice to carry with you throughout the year, noticing the invitations of spring, summer, fall, and winter and how each has its own quality and energy.

Notice what nature teaches you about the ebb and flow of life. Be mindful when your own anxious thoughts arise. When they do, see if you can ask nature to hold them for you as you breathe into spaciousness and surplus once again.

If you have a camera with you, stay open to receiving images of abundance without trying to capture things. Keep your stance open to the moment and what it brings.

When you return from your walk, allow some time in silence and sit and gaze on the images you received (whether in your imagination or on your camera) with an open and curious heart. In what ways is your heart's deeper hunger for abundance revealed?

DAY 6: IMAGINATIVE PRAYER

> *[Jesus] sat down opposite the treasury and watched*
> *the crowd putting money into the treasury. Many*
> *rich people put in large sums. A poor widow came*
> *and put in two small copper coins, which are worth*
> *a penny. Then he called his disciples and said to*
> *them, "Truly I tell you; this poor widow has put*
> *in more than all those who are contributing to the*
> *treasury. For all of them have contributed out of*
> *their abundance; but she out of her poverty has put*
> *in everything she had, all she had to live on."*
>   *The Widow's Gift (Mark 12:41–44)*

RETURN TO THE Scripture text for this week and read it through again slowly, with the ears of the heart. See yourself stepping into the scene with all your senses attuned and watch the scene unfold. You are there at the temple treasury with the crowds of people putting their money into the offering. You see many rich people pouring in large piles of coins. Imagine the buzz of energy, the different faces, the smells and sights. Notice how your body feels in this scene.

See the poor widow enter into this scene. Notice how she appears, her countenance, her energy. Watch as she carefully takes two copper coins and gives these as her offering. Notice Jesus and the disciples watching this scene as well and their responses to what is happening.

Stand among the disciples as Jesus teaches about the widow's generosity. Hear the words he speaks and really take them in. See what they mean for you in this moment of your life.

Engage in a conversation with members of the crowd, with the poor widow, with Jesus, and with each of the disciples. Imagine being the treasure, the bags of wealth, the two copper coins, an animal in the midst also observing. Spend some time noticing the details of the experience and how you feel in response. What makes you curious? Where do you want to ask questions? Where do you want to sit and simply savor?

Ask the widow for her wisdom. Let her speak to your own life circumstances and where you give from abundance and where from your poverty.

Once your exploration feels complete, spend some time writing this story down. What are the details you want to include? What did you discover?

DAY 7: CREATIVE RITUAL—EARTH MANDALA

I INVITE YOU to continue building your altar through these weeks, especially as you go on your contemplative walks and new symbols present themselves to you.

This week, I also invite you into a simple ritual of trust and surrender. You will want to go somewhere outdoors if possible, like a neighborhood park, a forest trail, or the seashore. You can also do this in a small nearby garden or if you have a yard, if preferable. Begin with some prayer and centering, asking the Spirit to guide you as you begin.

Gather some natural objects that have fallen to the ground (rather than picking anything off trees). Spend up to a half an hour looking for twigs, leaves, acorns, and other symbols. When you feel like you have "enough" bring them to a space on the ground, or a rock or tree stump, where you can create a mandala.

"Mandala" is a Sanskrit word for circle, and a mandala is a circular offering with a sacred intention. We find mandalas in rose windows, and Tibetan Buddhist monks create intricate mandalas made from colored sand, and once created, they then brush it all away. The psychologist Carl Jung said that whenever a mandala appeared in a client's dream it was a symbol for wholeness.

Create this mandala with a sacred intention using the natural objects you have found. Allow this act of creation to be a prayer. You might consider praying for deeper trust and a spirit of generosity. Once it has been completed, spend some time with it. Then eventually, when you have received its wisdom and invitation for you, walk away from it, leaving it to be swept away by wind and rain or wild creatures carrying pieces of it away. Let it be an offering to the world of creative joy, releasing your hold on having an end product. Relish how those who pass it by before it blows away might find their own moment of joy in it. Let this act of release be a claiming of trust.

Reflection Questions

Does your energy feel "mortgaged" into the future?

What forms of scarcity especially cause you anxiety?

How might you create some Sabbath time in your days or
   weeks?

What would a "store of energy" feel like for you?

What does "enough" look like for you? Enough time, enough
   money, enough love?

What does your hunger for enough feel like?

—————— **CLOSING BLESSING** ——————

Spirit of generous abundance,

remind us there is always more than enough,

enough food, enough love, enough time, enough resources.

Help us to see how our patterns of living in separation

and disconnection amplifies our scarcity.

Bring us into the joy and challenge of community

where bread divided multiplies, where laughter shared
overflows.

Empower us to share freely from our own abundance

with others in need. Slow us down to see how time expands

when we breathe and pay attention.

Bless us in our efforts to trust

in the goodness and love that pulses through the world

sustaining it moment by moment.

Give us the courage to speak out

when resources are distributed unfairly,

so we may remind others there is more to share.

Encourage us to release that which we no longer

need to hold onto so tightly.

Inspire us to live in a way that witnesses

to our trust in the lavish fullness of life.

Week 3

AN INVITATION TO
FAST FROM SPEED AND RUSHING

EMBRACE SLOWNESS
AND PAUSING

Week 3 Reflection

MODERN LIFE SEEMS to move at full speed and many of us can hardly catch our breath between the demands of earning a living, nurturing family and friendships, and the hundreds of small daily details like paying our bills, cleaning, and grocery shopping. More and more we feel stretched thin by commitments and lament our busyness, but without a clear sense of the alternative.

Our calendars may be full of appointments, work commitments, and social activities, heaving under the weight of expectations. Some of us may claim "busyness" as a point of pride. Certainly, in Western culture, busy is seen as the mark of a full and desirable life.

It can be challenging to know where to begin in dismantling this way of living. We may have people who depend on us, like children and aging parents. We may be terrified of slowing down and really listening to our lives. And yet so many of us are exhausted and depleted.

In *This Here Flesh*, Cole Arthur Riley writes:

> *Our societies and communities have a way of grinding up and serving out dignity in portions based on our own human ideals and idols. In the history of the white Western world, you can trace a perversion of dignity in the name of usefulness. You are no longer in the image of God, you are currency.*
>
> *We cannot help but entwine our concept of dignity with how much a person can do. The sick, the elderly, the disabled, the neurodivergent, my sweet cousin on the autism spectrum—we tend to assign a lesser social value to those whose "doing" cannot be enslaved in a given output. We should look to them as sacred guides out of the bondage of productivity. Instead we withhold social status and capital, we neglect to acknowledge that theirs is a liberation we can learn from.*

Rest, slowness, pausing are all pathways to a liberation of body and soul, not a reward for good work later on. It is a disruption of a system that would exploit our labor until we can work no longer, treating us, as Riley writes, like "currency." I love this image of those who are unable to "do" in a capitalistic, productive sense as "sacred guides" toward a liberation and restfulness that is ours by what theologian Tricia Hersey calls our divine "birthright."

What do the sacred guides you know teach you about liberation and dignity and how you might practice that in your environment? Maybe it's not heading off on a retreat to ponder new possibilities—but something much closer to home, in your environment. Where do you see opportunities for breathing spaces and slowness within your days? The monastic tradition invites us into the practice of stopping one thing before beginning another. It is the acknowledgment that in the space of transition and threshold is a sacred dimension, a holy pause full of possibility.

What might it be like to allow just a five-minute window to sit in silence between appointments? Or if, after finishing a phone call or checking your email, you take just five long, slow, deep breaths before pushing on to the next thing?

We often think of these in-between times as wasted moments and inconveniences, rather than opportunities to return again and again, to awaken to the gifts right here, not the ones we imagine waiting for us beyond the next door. But what if we built in these thresholds between our daily activities, just for a few minutes to intentionally savor silence and breath?

When we pause between activities or moments in our day, we open ourselves to the possibility of discovering a new kind of presence to the "in-between times." When we rush from one thing to another, we skim over the surface of life, losing that sacred attentiveness that brings forth revelations in the most ordinary of moments.

Theologian and mystic Howard Thurman writes in *Meditations of the Heart* that "One could not begin the cultivation of the prayer life at a more practical point than deliberately to seek each day, and several times a day, a lull in the rhythm of daily doing, a period when nothing happens that demands active participation." This lull of being, rather than doing, is a holy pause. He later writes: "The moment of pause, the point of rest, has its own magic." There is no other adequate substitute. No caffeinated beverages or other stimulants, no sleep-deprivation techniques can offer us the grace that a restful pause can.

We are continually crossing thresholds in our lives, both the literal kind when moving through doorways, leaving the building, or going to another room, and the metaphorical thresholds, when time becomes a transition space of waiting and tending. We hope for news about a friend struggling with illness; we are longing for clarity about our own deepest dreams. This place between is a place of stillness, where we let go of what came before and prepare ourselves to enter fully into what comes next.

The holy pause calls us to a sense of reverence for slowness, for mindfulness, and for the fertile dark spaces between our goals where we can pause and center ourselves, and listen.

We can open up a space within for God to work. We can become fully conscious of what we are about to do rather than mindlessly completing another task.

The holy pause can also be the space of integration and healing. When we rush through our lives, we often don't allow time to gather the pieces of ourselves so our fragmented selves can come together again. When we allow rest, we awaken to the broken places that often push us to keep doing and producing and striving. There are things in life best done slowly.

In *Staying Awake*, Tyler Sit offers this beautiful interpretation of the first creation story in Genesis. After working to create the universe, "then She rested."

> *God discovered a point at which, even in Her*
> *infinite expansiveness, even with all of Creation*
> *bowing to Her every word, even as* the author of
> time itself, *She took a break.*
>
> *And God didn't apologize for it; She wasn't*
> *dramatic about it. She rested because She wanted*
> *to rest, plain and simple.* Then *She blessed that day*
> *and made it holy (Genesis 2:3). Holy! All the other*
> *days She calls "good" but the Day of Rest is holy.*

Sabbath is for me the most vital of all spiritual practices, precisely because of how it forces me to disrupt Empire-based centering of work and productivity and allows me to taste another world and way of being. We are called to shift our priorities so that we center resting in God as the primary focus of our lives, instead of using work as our starting point in considering what is valuable.

This week you are invited to fast from rushing through life and overscheduling your commitments. Offer yourself the gift of pausing before and after appointments whenever possible, to simply savor the sheer grace of the moment. You may experience a restlessness in these times between; you may need to slow your body and mind down with slow breathing. Often, we are caught up in overstimulation and our bodies are holding anxiety. Doing helps to relieve that, but may also lead us to exhaustion and burnout.

The desert way also calls us to value holy leisure, times when we are not directing our attention on achieving anything, but simply resting in the goodness of the divine. Consider embracing the practice of resting, doing nothing at all, making room for God to erupt in new ways in the spaces between.

Daily Practices

DAY 1: *LECTIO DIVINA*

> *Every day [Jesus] was teaching in the temple, and*
> *at night he would go out and spend the night on the*
> *Mount of Olives, as it was called. And all the people*
> *would get up early in the morning to listen to him*
> *in the temple.*
> *Jesus on the Mount of Olives (Luke 21:37–38)*

I LOVE THIS subtle short passage which tells us that while every day Jesus goes to teach in the temple, he also goes to spend each night in a place of retreat and rest, on the Mount of Olives. His pattern of being in the world witnesses a sacred rhythm of rest and work. He knew the necessity of replenishing his reservoir of energy.

As a faithful Jew, Jesus would also have had a discipline of Sabbath observance. While he did sometimes perform miracles of healing on the Sabbath, much to the consternation of the Pharisees, he would also have honored one day each week as a time to cease from effort and striving. He would have followed God's commandment to stop laboring from sunset to sunset on Shabbat to savor the delights of rest and savor the beauty of a world made by a Creator who proclaimed it all as so very good.

Spend some time in sacred reading with this passage and listen for the word or phrase that shimmers, then let it unfold in your imagination. Finally, make space for the sacred invitation to your own life to arrive. Rest into silence at the end and spend a few minutes journaling anything you noticed or discovered.

DAY 2: BREATH PRAYER—I LET GO AND REST

BREATH CAN BE such a support in helping us to rest deeply and fast from our need to do in order to feel accomplished. In a world that prizes doing and busyness, to allow a few minutes each day to breathe is an act of courage and resistance. It is a way to say that this is core to who we are as beings made of body and soul.

Breath also has a physiological effect on our parasympathetic nervous system. Slow breathing can slow us down physically and ease our bodies' anxiety.

Create a space to really drop into this prayer and allow your body to release with each exhale. You might begin by taking a few exaggerated breaths where you exhale with a loud sigh. This practice can really amplify any release your breath facilitates in your body. Then continue by moving into this breath prayer.

Breathe in: I let go

Breathe out: And rest

With each inhale as you whisper, "I let go," see if there are beliefs, habits, and commitments you can actively let go of. You might especially focus on any compulsions to stay busy and overcommitted. With each exhale, whisper "and rest" and allow your body to soften even further.

As you deepen into the invitation to rest, imagine you are being held by the arms of the Beloved. There is nothing you need to *do* here, simply *be* and breathe.

DAY 3: *VISIO DIVINA*

I INVITE YOU to pray with the block print image by artist Kreg Yingst that opens this chapter. Take a few minutes to slow your breathing and center yourself in your heart. Soften your gaze and let your eyes wander around the image.

See the clouds above, the rolling hills with trees, the long undulating pathways stretching across fields, the tiny sanctuary space with enough room to find a quiet retreat from the busyness of life.

Imagine yourself walking those paths each day like Jesus in a sacred rhythm of evening restoration and then service to others in the day. See the inhale and exhale of your breath mirroring this cycle. Let your breath take you deeper into the image. Notice how you feel walking among the trees, under the clouds, across fields, and finally to rest. See if there is a moment in the image that especially calls to you in some way and pause there to take it in.

Make space within for any images, feelings, or memories that arise. Ask what the invitation being offered to you in this prayer might be. Listen for how you are being called through these images.

If you feel comfortable, close your eyes and rest into silence for a few moments. Let yourself become still in mind and heart.

When you open your eyes, gaze again at the image and see if there is anything else you notice. How does this image support your call to fast from speed and rushing and to embrace slowness? Allow some time to write any insights or discoveries.

DAY 4: MEDITATION WITH THE DESERT ELDERS

A hunter in the desert saw Abba Anthony enjoying himself with the brethren and he was shocked. Wanting to show him that it was necessary sometimes to meet the needs of the brethren, the old man said to him, "Put an arrow in your bow and shoot it." So he did. The old man said, "Shoot another," and he did so. Then the old man said "Shoot yet again," and the hunter replied "If I bend my bow so much I will break it." Then the old man said to him, "It is the same with the work of God. If we stretch the brethren beyond measure they will soon break. Sometimes it is necessary to come down to meet their needs." When he heard these words the hunter was pierced with compunction and, greatly edified by the old man, he went away. As for the brethren, they went home strengthened. (Anthony 13)

WHILE THE DESERT mothers and fathers write extensively about diligence and discipline in the spiritual life, there are also some wonderful stories that remind us about the need to give rest to the body and soul. We live in a world that wants us to shoot arrows from our bow again and again, without regard for how stretched we feel, how close to breaking we often come with the multiple demands placed upon us.

Western culture prizes productivity and busyness. We strive after accomplishments and checking things off our lists. So little of it truly satisfies us.

Just as Jesus took regular time for rest and slowness, so too the desert elders valued a slow rhythm of life. They weren't in a rush to get anywhere because they trusted in the long, slow unfolding of time. They knew spiritual transformation was not a race.

Allow some time to center yourself and breathe deeply. Slow yourself and your thoughts down as much as possible. Rest for a while with the sacred presence within your heart.

Welcome in Abba Anthony to be present with you. Notice how he appears. Listen to him tell you this story again about the hunter in the desert. Share with him the ways you bend your bow too much.

What are the ways you long to enjoy yourself the way the abba and his fellow brothers were? Share your desire for holy leisure. See what wisdom he has to offer. Ask him to bless this longing for slowness and rest you have.

Imagine he gifts you with a small snail shell and in the spiral of it you see the invitation to move slowly and retreat when needed.

When you have listened to Abba Anthony's wisdom for a while, offer gratitude for his presence. Return gently to the room you are in and spend some time in reflection.

DAY 5: CONTEMPLATIVE WALK

AS YOU GO out on your contemplative walk this week, I invite you to really emphasize the slow aspect of this practice. This is less about your walking speed and more about our ability to tune in and pay attention to the unfolding of each moment, without letting ourselves get distracted, perhaps by creating lists in our mind of things to do later or setting a goal for ourselves in how far we might walk or how many steps are recorded on our fitness tracker.

While you walk in the world, open yourself to notice signs of slowness and rest in nature. Open yourself to the ways that nature invites you to move at a different pace.

What are the images and symbols that offer a window for you into the rhythm of creating and resting that is at the heart of the natural world? If you have your camera, be open to receiving images of slowness as gift.

When you return from your walk allow some time in silence and sit and gaze on the images you received (whether in your imagination or on your camera) with an open and curious heart. In what ways is your heart's deeper hunger for slowness revealed?

DAY 6: IMAGINATIVE PRAYER

Every day [Jesus] was teaching in the temple, and
at night he would go out and spend the night on the
Mount of Olives, as it was called. And all the people
would get up early in the morning to listen to him
in the temple.
Jesus on the Mount of Olives (Luke 21:37–38)

READ THE SCRIPTURE passage for this week again. Enter into
the scene with all your senses attuned. See yourself compan-
ioning Jesus as he teaches in the temple. Listen for his words
of wisdom.

As night approaches, ask if you can walk with him up to
the Mount of Olives. Engage him in conversation about the
holy rhythms of his life and what sustains him in his work of
teaching and healing.

As you walk together, notice what you smell, the sounds
around you, the colors and hues. Reach out and touch things
around you to experience their textures.

When you reach Jesus's destination, rest with him there
for a little while. Notice his countenance and how it shifts
in this place. Continue any conversation you'd like to have.
Engage in dialogue with the pathway, with the mount itself,
with the trees or any birds flying about. Open your heart to
how these elements of the setting might speak to you in your
life right now.

Eventually allow yourself to simply rest with Jesus in silence. Give space for the deep quiet of the growing night. See what new sounds arise around you and within you.

Experience the gift and grace of sleep there, in a place withdrawn from the busyness of the world. Notice how you feel upon awakening and when it is time to return to the temple to teach again.

When the experience feels complete, allow some time to journal or draw any discoveries you made in this prayer.

DAY 7: CREATIVE RITUAL FOR SABBATH

CREATE A RITUAL this week for a Sabbath practice of your own. If you already have a Sabbath practice, consider deepening into it, inspired by what you are noticing and discovering through this week's focus.

First decide on a day and time for Sabbath. You might choose a full day, or you might begin with a shorter period of time like a Sabbath morning or afternoon. Choose a reading or write a blessing for this chapter (or use the blessing offered at the end of this section). Listen to a piece of music that slows you down and helps you to become more present.

You might also want to incorporate some ritual actions, like turning off your computer or placing your phone into a special box so that you unplug from technology.

Let the start and end of your Sabbath time be marked by a ritual that honors these moments as a time of deep restfulness. This could be as simple as lighting a candle or saying a short prayer. Then decide what activities would feel especially restful. Perhaps some journaling about the week that has passed or a walk in a nearby woodland. Maybe a nap or time sitting in silence. You might want to cook a nourishing meal. Whatever you choose, check in to make sure these are things that bring you pleasure and rest and are not part of checking something off a list of things to do.

Reflection Questions

What are the ways you push forward in your life, even when
   tired or depleted?

What is your own Mount of Olives?

What are the places and moments when you can breathe more
   slowly?

How can you make your days more restful?

What are the commitments in your life you could release to
   make more space for being?

What has been your previous experience with Sabbath
   rhythms?

What does your true hunger for rest reveal to you about your
   life?

--- **CLOSING BLESSING** ---

Holy One, you call us to the lavish gift of rest.

Support us as we lay aside our tasks, our plans, our worries

and turn to you with open hearts.

Whisper to us in the silence

of your love for us, simply for who we are.

Bless us with the deep renewal

that rest brings and transform our daily patterns

so we might weave Sabbath into every day.

Slow us down when our minds race,

when our calendars overflow with demands,

when our hearts flutter with overwhelm.

Hold us in that holy pause,

reveal to us again the beauty of this world,

of steam rising from coffee,

of the dog's pleading eyes, of the rose blooming.

Help us to see how everything in creation

takes its time, no rushing, no pushing.

In that open space gather all of our scattered

parts together into the wholeness

of who we were created to be.

Week 4

AN INVITATION TO
FAST FROM HOLDING
IT ALL TOGETHER

EMBRACE TENDERNESS
AND VULNERABILITY

Week 4 Reflection

IN 2003, MY mother became seriously ill quite suddenly and died a few days later in the ICU. I was only thirty-three at the time, she was my second parent to die, and I had no siblings. I was left with a profound aloneness, even with my beloved husband's faithful companionship. We had recently moved to Seattle from the San Francisco Bay area, so I didn't have close friends nearby either. At first, I coped in the way that had always served me well. By being strong and holding everything together, keeping busy when I could so that I could distract myself from the tremendous grief.

Western culture rewards us greatly for being able to pull ourselves together and carry on with life in the face of loss and sorrow. Speed, productivity, and a denial of difficult emotions are the hallmark of our times. In our rush to get things done we armor ourselves even more. We build internal walls to help keep the grief from spilling over into our days. We build external walls in our bodies that reflect this inner rigidity.

The problem was that—as sometimes happens when we try to hold back the deluge of emotion for too long—I became ill. It started with a number of vague things like fatigue, headaches, depression, skin rashes. I visited doctors, chiropractors, herbalists, energy workers, and other kinds of healers. None of these remedies fully alleviated my pain and discomfort.

During this time, I discovered a practice called yin yoga, in which seated or lying postures are held for three to five minutes with the aim of softening the connective tissues. At first, I found it so hard to stay still and be, but I slowly grew to love this time of sitting with my body and paying attention to the places of holding, of physical armoring, of tightness and tension. Breathing into these places with loving attention brought a great softening to my body. And in the midst of that softening other things began to loosen their grip—including my holding back of the grief I feared would drown me as my heart opened to the river of mourning and demanded my attention. Without bidding, tears arose and I learned to welcome them in.

A wonderful spiritual director also helped guide me through this territory of savage grief. I took long contemplative walks and let the turning of the seasons become a scripture text for me, speaking of the necessity of autumn's release and winter's rest alongside of spring's blossoming and summer's fruitfulness.

In the early Christian desert tradition, softening was the fruit of committed prayer and practice. And tears were considered a gift, shed over our grief at loss but also at the places in our lives that had become hardened, ways we had turned away from God.

One type of tears are *penthos*, tears of compunction, a puncturing of the hard shell of the heart, which pierces to our core, reminding us of who we most deeply are. This "gift of tears," as they are sometimes referred to, reveals to us the misguided perfectionism, games, and manipulations we struggle to achieve, as well as the stories we tell ourselves. These tears free us from lying and any form of pretense that takes over when we feel anxious or sad.

Theologian John Chryssavgis writes: "Tears and weeping indicate a significant frontier in the way of the desert. They bespeak a promise. In fact, they are the only way into the heart." This frontier is the boundary between our old ways of seeing and believing and the wide new expansiveness into which contemplative prayer calls us. Compunction awakens us to all the ways we have been false to our own deepest self and to the profound longing that is kindled when we pay attention to the heart.

The "gift of tears" written about by the desert elders also is celebrated several centuries later by Spanish mystic St.

Ignatius of Loyola. These tears, he says, are not about finding a reason for our pain and suffering. They do not give answers but instead call us to a deep attentiveness to the longings of our heart. They continue to flow until we drop our masks and self-deception and return to the source of our lives and longing. They are a sign that we have crossed a threshold into a profound sense of humility. Humility is a practice of remembering we come from Earth and to Earth we will one day return. This sign and this humility help us to hold our griefs and losses with great tenderness and compassion.

In the Christian Scriptures we find Jesus weeping over the death of his friend Lazarus and over the city of Jerusalem. Certainly, his final hours nailed to a cross crying out "my God, my God, why have you abandoned me?" were a profound witness to the call of radical vulnerability as a portal to divine grace.

We seek and feel God in the places of pain and sorrow, in the places of paradox and contradiction. Our tears can reveal our deepest gratitude when we acknowledge that we cannot possess anything that is a gift to us, neither the spring blossoming nor our partner in life. We learn to love without holding on. The times my marriage has bloomed even further have often been the times of shared vulnerability, when we allow ourselves to reveal our soft underbellies to one another. In the time of my almost thirty years with my husband, we have experienced all four of our parents dying, each loss a fresh sorrow to make space for and walk together tenderly through those deserts.

Humility was essential to the desert elders in overcoming what they described as demons. Demons were essentially a metaphor for the things that vex and challenge us and break our hearts. Amma Theodora wrote, "Nothing can overcome us, but only humility." "Do you see how humility is victorious over demons?" (Theodora 6). Humility is a way of consciously bringing ourselves into relationship with all that is tender and vulnerable within ourselves and honoring our humanity.

I am reminded again of the seductiveness of strength, of pretending that everything feels fine when I am struggling inside. How others mumble and pull away sometimes when I reveal my grieving persists, when they think I should be over it. How the demands of work continue to call, asking me to push through.

I also remember that the places of the greatest disruptions in my life have surprisingly been, too, the occasions of the most profound gifts. The seasons when I have allowed myself to feel my broken heart, and to know my woundedness, are the times when my compassion for the world has deepened beyond my previous capacity.

Tyler Sit writes about this as well, in *Staying Awake*, describing this resistance to vulnerability as a form of toxic masculinity in our culture: "when we men weaponize stereotypes of masculinity (like being forceful or unfeeling) to perilous effect on other people, the planet, and ourselves." He goes on to highlight how toxic masculinity is so pervasive it is hard to see it and churches often reinforce it. It affects women and men both. This culture of strength and aggressiveness means we bypass our grief and never allow it space so we can move toward healing. Our pain then becomes directed in other ways and our lives and relationships suffer.

The Lenten discipline for this week is to allow a great softening this season and, in the fertile earth of your heart, to see what begins to sprout there that never had a chance in the hardened soil.

As you practice a fast from strength, you learn to let go of the ways you've tried to hold everything together. Resist the demand to continue pushing when everything in your body and heart cries out to pause. Give space for the exquisite vulnerability of being human.

Daily Practices

DAY 1: *LECTIO DIVINA*

> *When Mary came where Jesus was and saw him, she*
> *knelt at his feet and said to him, "Lord, if you had*
> *been here, my brother would not have died." When*
> *Jesus saw her weeping and the Jews who came with*
> *her also weeping, he was greatly disturbed in spirit*
> *and deeply moved. He said, "Where have you laid*
> *him?" They said to him, "Lord, come and see." Jesus*
> *began to weep.*
>
> > *The Death of Lazarus (John 11:32–35)*

WHEN JESUS'S FRIEND Lazarus died, Jesus came to be with the family. He met Mary, who was weeping, the others with her were weeping, and Jesus started to weep as well. This may seem odd given that in the story he is about to raise Lazarus from the dead. Why weep when a miracle is about to happen to reverse the grief they are experiencing?

Perhaps because Jesus knows that tears can be a gateway to the holy. Maybe it is only through his tears that he summons the strength for what comes next. So often we try to hold it all together while we are crumbling inside. Our culture doesn't create space to allow us to fall apart. Here is a community feeling the loss of a friend and family member. The resurrection to come does not relieve the need for weeping now.

Enter into prayer with this passage through the practice of *lectio divina* and open to a word or phrase, letting that expand in your heart. See what shimmers for you. See what you discover and the invitations that emerge.

DAY 2: BREATH PRAYER—LET MY WEEPING FLOW FREELY

THE INVITATION THIS week is to fast from always being strong and holding it all together, which means it is also an invitation to allow ourselves to weep freely if needed. We each have a different relationship to tears, so if tears are challenging for you to access, there is no need to berate yourself for not being able to cry easily. But accept the invitation to sit with the grief and make space for whatever comes.

Some may have easy access to tears. I am someone who cries quite easily. Sometimes over personal loss and grief, sometimes over global events. Often, I cry when listening to music or watching a movie and don't even know exactly what the source of my tears is. I just know they are holy so I try to make space for them.

If weeping feels difficult, notice how your body responds to this space for grieving. Connect to the place where you feel the sorrow moving in you; this might be your heart, your gut, or another place. Place a hand here as a gesture of support and care for yourself.

In your breath prayer this week, you are invited to offer an invocation and permission for your tears to flow freely. Sometimes the simple act of permission can open up a channel in us that we didn't even realize we were blocking off.

Breathe in: Let my weeping
Breathe out: Flow freely

As you inhale, say quietly, "Let my weeping," and see if you can connect to the source of tears within you and see them as a sacred gift. As you exhale, say, "flow freely," and allow your body to soften and surrender into that exhalation. As you breathe out imagine making space for the tears to flow where they didn't have room before.

Sit like this for ten minutes, simply allowing room for grief to emerge and be expressed if needed. If there is nothing personal to connect to, you can always invite tears for the suffering of a friend or for devastating need within global events.

If at any time you feel overwhelmed by your tears, return to your body, feel your feet on the ground and quiet your breathing, releasing words and images. Look around the room and name the things you see. This is a helpful way to reconnect if you start to feel lost.

If tears do not come, simply sit with the feelings and sensations arising, trusting them as an expression of grief.

Allow this space to be a sacred gift to your tender heart, to feel the fragility and vulnerability of human life and offer your tears as a blessing.

DAY 3: *VISIO DIVINA*

I INVITE YOU to pray with the block print image by artist Kreg Yingst that opens this chapter. Spend some time breathing slowly and deeply, and softening your gaze.

Bring eyes of curiosity and compassion to the image. Let your gaze wander around the artwork, noticing the lines and shapes and textures. See Jesus's face, eyes closed, tears streaming down. Enter into his moment of sorrow with him.

Follow the encircling of arms as Jesus embraces another in this tender exchange. See the texture of their cloaks and the white space around them.

Notice where your eyes want to rest in this image and spend some time lingering there. See what is stirred in your heart, making room for images, feelings, and memories. Be especially present to your own places of vulnerability and tenderness. Ask what the invitation is for you in this season of your life.

Release images and words for a few moments and breathe into the silence. Close your eyes if you feel comfortable, and simply rest.

When you open your eyes again, gaze upon the image one more time and see what you notice now. How does this image support you in the call to fast from strength and embrace tenderness? Spend some time writing or drawing what you discovered.

DAY 4: MEDITATION WITH THE DESERT ELDERS

> *It was said of (Abba Arsenius) that he had a hollow*
> *in his chest channeled out by the tears which fell*
> *from his eyes all his life while he sat at his manual*
> *work. When Abba Poemen learned that he was*
> *dead, he said weeping, "Truly you are blessed, Abba*
> *Arsenius, for you wept for yourself and this world."*
> *(Arsenius 41)*

FOR ABBA ARSENIUS, tears were a welcome gift and a sign that healing and transformation were taking place. As the spiritual path is lifelong, so too for him was the opening of the heart to tears.

As you spend some time meditating on this story, find a quiet place and slow your breathing down. Descend into the cave of your heart. Rest there for a few moments with the Holy One, simply being.

Welcome in the presence again of Abba Arsenius, one of the desert fathers we prayed with earlier. Read the story above two or three times. Sit with this monk weeping freely and see his tears as an essential aspect of the spiritual path. See his chest hollowed in like a smooth stone from the tears he has shed. Share with him some of the things you grieve for in your life. Sit and weep together for a while.

Reflect on the ways you try to hold everything together and be strong. Reflect on the times in your life when you resist asking for help or support from a loved one, a friend, or even God. See if you might try to consciously soften yourself through your breathing, yielding gently into the Love available to you.

Ask Abba Arsenius to bless you in your weeping, to let your tears bathe you in grace. Notice what it is like to be witnessed in this way. Imagine as he reaches toward you, he hands you a gift, a small blue glass bottle with the words from Psalm 56:8 etched into it: "You have collected all my tears in a bottle." You receive the gift with gratitude and savor it for a few moments.

When you are ready, slowly return to the room and allow some time to reflect on what you experienced.

DAY 5: CONTEMPLATIVE WALK

AS YOU WALK today, keep this week's theme close to heart. Notice how the world around you responds to this invitation to fast from being strong and open to the tenderness of tears. How does grief meet you in the symbols that show up along the way? How does nature offer you support for your tears? These aren't questions to answer so much as live into as you walk.

Pay attention to anything that "shimmers" for you or calls to you in some way. There might be a stone on your path or a leaf fluttering in the wind that speaks to the grief you carry. Perhaps it is simply in the sound of the wind that you feel met by the world. How does nature meet you in your grief?

Allow some time for journaling when you return, to make note of anything you noticed or discovered. This is not a time to try to figure anything out, but to be present to your experience and what moved your heart during this time.

DAY 6: IMAGINATIVE PRAYER

When Mary came where Jesus was and saw him, she knelt at his feet and said to him, "Lord, if you had been here, my brother would not have died." When Jesus saw her weeping and the Jews who came with her also weeping, he was greatly disturbed in spirit and deeply moved. He said, "Where have you laid him?" They said to him, "Lord, come and see." Jesus began to weep.

The Death of Lazarus (John 11:32–35)

READ THE SCRIPTURE passage for this week through again slowly. Imagine yourself stepping into the scene and being there with Mary, Jesus, and the others. Open your senses to the experience. See Mary kneeling before Jesus and sharing with him about her brother Lazarus. Hear the sobbing around you and as Jesus himself begins to weep openly.

Notice the place you are in, its smells and sights. See how people are dressed. Attune to their experience of grief.

Enter into dialogue with Jesus about his grief. Ask him to share with you the source of his tears. See if he has wisdom for you about your own places of grieving. Speak with Mary and the others present about what they are feeling right now. Make space for silence between the words.

Experience the scene from different perspectives. You might imagine you are a chair holding up a grief-stricken woman. Or a jug of water on the table to quench thirst. Or a small animal observing things from the side. Be curious and notice the places that stir you to question and engage.

Let the scene continue to unfold, making space for what wants to emerge. Then write the story that is being told in the cracks between the words told in the Scripture. How would you describe what is happening within and around you?

DAY 7: CREATIVE RITUAL FOR GRIEF

THERE IS SUCH a gift when we are met in our grief by someone who can hold the space for us and witness us without
needing to change anything. When my mother died the grief
was overwhelming. I had gone through a major life transition
and I wasn't sure how I was going to hold things together and
manage life.

That I had a wise spiritual director to sit with me in my
grief opened something in me. He sat with me in my grief. He
never tried to hurry me along. In fact, he suggested I create a
daily ritual for mourning my loss. What this meant was that
I would set aside time each day, usually about a half an hour,
to really allow my grief to have full expression. It became part
of my sacred practice, and in those times I discovered how
profoundly grief speaks to the love we carry for those we lost.

In giving myself room to grieve in a ritual way and time,
another grace emerged: I was able to manage better in the rest
of my life. I still had moments when tears erupted unexpect-
edly, but I wasn't trying to hold it together all of the time.
Allowing myself this space to grieve intentionally helped me
to process my loss in a deeper way.

You may have a specific loss you are grieving: the loss of
a loved one, the loss of an ability, the loss of a dream. Or it
might be a grief that is less personal, maybe the losses caused
by climate chaos or the extinction of species, or the cost of
war, or the painful oppression of poverty. For this week choose

one thing to grieve, or better yet, let it choose you. Ask what your heart is weeping most loudly for and offer it space for this sacred task.

Steps for a Grief Ritual

To do this, find a time when you will not be disturbed. Turn off your phone and notifications.

Sit or lie down in a comfortable place. You might want to light a candle as a way to ritualize this time.

Offer a prayer to God, who weeps with you, and ask to be held in this sacred time and space.

Quiet your heart to listen for what is true for you today around any grief you are holding.

Allow the feelings to rise and fall as needed.

At the end of this time offer a prayer of gratitude for the gift of tears. Give thanks for the blessing of love in your life that opens up the heart of grief.

Reflection Questions

What is your relationship to weeping? Do you cry freely or
hold back tears?

What are the ways you try to avoid feeling your sorrow? What
are your coping mechanisms?

What are the griefs you still carry? How might you make space
to honor these?

When you notice the impulse to be strong and hold everything
together, what are the practices that help you to soften
toward yourself?

When you touch into your true hunger for authentic
expression, what do you discover there?

CLOSING BLESSING

Midwife of our weeping,

hold us in our times of grief and loss,

be with us as we give expression to our love.

Bathe us in the brine of healing,

gather our tears in your vial,

wash us clean.

When we reach for strength and resist our sorrow

be a sanctuary for us, show us the river of our sobs

and the great sea of collective grief it meets.

Let wave upon wave carry us

to the shores of your Love.

Remind us we are not alone in our sense of loss,

sanctify our tender places,

make holy our humanity.

Help us to know

grief and joy as sisters,

how loss carves us out,

making room one day

for a newfound delight.

Week 5

AN INVITATION TO
FAST FROM PLANNING
AND DEADLINES

EMBRACE UNFOLDING
AND RIPENING

Week 5 Reflection

I CONSIDER MYSELF a recovering planner. Recover-*ing* as it is a process. I will be the first to admit that my organizational skills are of great benefit to many aspects of my life and work. My gifts include holding big visions for the future. As someone who stewards a virtual monastery, there is much planning that goes into our programs. As a writer, I find deadlines extraordinarily helpful to be able to bring manuscripts to completion.

But planning can also be an act of trying to control life. It can get in the way of tending to how things actually want to unfold and ripen. My mind is often filled with plans and details and agendas. This can get quite noisy and keeps me from listening fully to how the Holy One is actually speaking into my life, what the divine presence desires for me in this season of my life.

Perhaps you have felt this too? It can be subtle, the way our minds are always moving into the future with their imagined perspectives. When we're always making plans for what we want to have happen, we lose the opportunity to pay attention to the bigger moments that call us to something we could not have imagined. Planning exerts a subtle direction on the trajectory of our lives. But life is often calling us to bigger things than our planning mind wants. And that internal chatter distracts us from the new visions breaking through.

The desert elders embraced something that moved the chatter away. The silence of the desert is what the elders called *hesychia*, which means stillness and silence. However, it is much deeper than just an external quiet. A person can live alone and still experience much noise within and a person can live amid a crowd and have a true sense of stillness in their heart. *Hesychia* has to do with our interior stillness.

> It was said of Abba Agathon that for three years he
> lived with a stone in his mouth, until he had learnt
> to keep silence. (Agathon 15)

There are many stories like this of the desert monks valuing silence as a way to hear the sacred shimmering in their lives.

Silence is the primordial sound of God speaking into our lives beneath the hum of everyday chatter. This chatter is often a form of planning ahead, whether anticipating an event or conversation, scheduling meetings, making to-do lists, or other forms of trying to direct the future. Silence helps us to rest for a while and let go of this continual hum of the mind's doing.

There is always a shadow side to silence—the kind of silence that keeps hidden secrets and abuses. This is not the life-giving silence the desert elders seek. Silence can be poisonous, as when someone's voice is being silenced or when we silence ourselves out of resentment or anger. Think of times when you have engaged silence as a weapon in a relationship. There is also the silence of hopelessness or giving up, feeling overwhelmed by life. Or silence that comes when we feel another has all the answers and our voice doesn't matter.

The desert monks are talking about silence that is life-giving. They urge us to seek a particular quality of silence that is attentive and emerges from a place of calm and peace. Our freedom to be silent in this way indicates our freedom from resentment and its power over us. Authentic silence is very challenging to achieve.

When we experience moments where we find ourselves releasing words and simply entering into an experience of wonder and beholding, this is the silence of God, moments when we are arrested by life's beauty.

Silence is challenging. We create all kinds of distractions and noise in our lives so we can avoid it. Thomas Merton writes about people who go to church and lead good lives but struggle with quiet:

> *Interior solitude is impossible for them. They fear it. They do everything they can to escape it. What is worse, they try to draw everyone else into activities as senseless and as devouring as their own. They are great promoters of useless work. They love to organize meetings and banquets and conferences and lectures. They print circulars, write letters, talk for hours on the telephone in order that they may gather a hundred people together in a large room where they will all fill the air with smoke and make a great deal of noise and roar at one another and clap their hands and stagger home at last patting one another on the back with the assurance that they have all done great things to spread the Kingdom of God.*

Merton is fierce in his critique of all the ways we cling to words to feel productive, while never making space to surrender into the unknowing of silence, experiencing silence as beyond all of our good words and intentions. Silence is what makes our actions meaningful, not the other way around.

Silence encourages us to release our desire to control the outcomes of everything and enter into the organic stillness from which new fruit can arise. When we rush and spread ourselves between too many commitments, and saturate our lives with noise, it becomes impossible to truly hear.

When I am immersed in planning my life, writing list after list of things to do, and always trying to meet the next deadline, I am called to pause from these things. The great Source of Silence invites me to soften my grip and pay attention to how life is actually arising. Sometimes we are so busy making plans and directing our lives, we forget there is a greater wisdom at work already nurturing new life for us.

In *The Seeker and the Monk*, Sophfronia Scott describes a powerful experience of allowing things to unfold of their own accord. She was staying at the Abbey of Gethsemani and wanted to walk to the lake to experience the wonder of nature that so captivated Merton in his life there. She was scheduled to return in time for lunch at the monastery, but then found herself called to keep going into the forest despite her initial plans, as she found herself giving in "to this silence." Scott writes: "I didn't know how far I was going, and it didn't matter—I had surrendered to whatever would come next." How often do we release the hold our plans have on us to yield to what is happening in the moment and give it space to unfold?

She continues on, "Connecting to divine spirit requires surrender. Giving myself over to the silence meant I would surrender control of my footsteps, my plans, and all expectations." In a world in which knowing where we are going is prized, where New Year's is always filled with marketing about setting goals and resolutions, letting ourselves get "lost" feels frightening and counter-cultural.

Being out in nature can help us with this release of agendas as creation follows its own rhythm and invites us to follow the rising and falling, the expansion and contraction, rather than our artificially constructed image of what our lives should look like. Theologian Randy Woodley also describes an experience of going out into nature to find a place to rest and surrender to this holding. In *Becoming Rooted*, he writes: "Great Mystery unscrews the tight lids of certainty that you hold too tightly, too fiercely. You realize, sometimes even trembling, that something greater than yourself is meeting you."

This week, you are invited to fast from your desire to control the direction of your life. Open yourself to the grace of silence, in which beauty comes alive and there are things already ripening and unfolding. From this space a garden can flourish.

Daily Practices

DAY 1: *LECTIO DIVINA*

> *I am the true vine, and my Father is the vinegrower.*
> *He removes every branch in me that bears no fruit.*
> *Every branch that bears fruit he prunes to make it*
> *bear more fruit. You have already been cleansed by*
> *the word that I have spoken to you. Abide in me as*
> *I abide in you. Just as the branch cannot bear fruit*
> *by itself unless it abides in the vine, neither can you*
> *unless you abide in me. I am the vine; you are the*
> *branches. Those who abide in me and I in them*
> *bear much fruit, because apart from me you can do*
> *nothing.*
>
> Jesus, the True Vine (John 15:1–5)

IN THE SILENCE we have space to see things in new ways. When we release our plans, we can begin to see how we are already unfolding to our true calling. Rather than picking the fruit too soon, when we make space to listen, we can see the process of ripening within us and notice when it is coming toward fullness.

In this passage, Jesus is reminding us of our organic nature. How we are rooted in something much greater than ourselves, and this rooting gives us the nourishment we need to unfurl into the world. This unfurling has the divine presence as its source and direction. So often we are driven by what constricts us rather than opening ourselves up: calendars needing filling or seeking a sense of accomplishment at getting things done.

As you pray with this passage from the gospel of John, attune yourself to the organic unfolding of your own soul. Pay attention to your own desires for planning and how they might be an effort to control the outcome of a particular situation. Allow room for holiness to erupt into your agenda.

DAY 2: BREATH PRAYER—I AM EMERGING FROM THE SACRED SOURCE

BREATHING IS AN organic process, meaning it happens naturally and unfolds in varying rhythms. Sometimes it is short and labored, sometimes long and steady. We can bring our intention to it to slow it down and create an inner spaciousness. Breath can help to still our hearts.

This breath prayer invites you to sit with the image from the Scripture of being a branch on God's vine. Allow this practice to deepen your commitment to your own slow ripening.

Breathe in: I am emerging
Breathe out: From the Sacred Source

As you inhale and say the words "I am emerging," see yourself as a tendril, a green shoot always growing and reaching. As you exhale and say the words "from the Sacred Source," see the holy vine from which you grow and are nourished.

With each breath, deepen into this image of yourself emerging from the Sacred Source. Notice how your body feels when you are aware of how you are so powerfully rooted.

DAY 3: *VISIO DIVINA*

I INVITE YOU to pray with the block print image by artist Kreg Yingst that opens this chapter. Begin by slowing your breath and softening your body. Bring your attention present and your gaze to the image.

Let your eyes wander around the image. Take in the vine, roots, leaves, fruit, and soil. Notice the white space holding it all. Follow the root to the top of the vine. Notice the textures. See what aspect of the image is calling to you for closer attention and pondering.

Let your eyes rest there for a little while and become aware of any feelings, images, or memories that arise in response. Make room for this prayer to ripen in your heart. Listen for the sense of invitation that is arising. What new awareness is this image calling you to consider in this season of your life?

Let go, for a moment, of words and images and rest into stillness. Breathe slowly and gently, becoming aware of being sustained by Spirit moment by moment. Savor this for a little while.

When your gaze returns to the image, take it in as a whole once more and see what you notice. How does this image support you in the call to fast from planning and embrace your own slow ripening? Spend some time journaling or drawing in response.

DAY 4: MEDITATION WITH THE DESERT ELDERS

> *It was said of Abba John that he withdrew and lived
> in the desert at Scetis with an old man of Thebes.
> His abba, taking a piece of dry wood, planted it,
> and said to him, "Water it every day with a bottle of
> water, until it bears fruit." Now the water was so far
> away that he had to leave in the evening and return
> the following morning. At the end of three years the
> wood came to life and bore fruit. Then the old man
> took some of the fruit and carried it to the church
> saying to the brethren, "Take and eat the fruit of
> obedience." (John 1)*

SHOWING UP EACH day and staying committed to our practice is the desert way. This is the wisdom teaching from Abba
John, when our tendency is to plan and predict.

The commitment to practice, even without the visible evidence of results, brings us back to the detachment of
apatheia—not being attached to the results of our practice.
When we continually begin again, the fruit will come with
time. Walking for miles each day to water something that took
three years to bear fruit must have demanded an extraordi-
nary amount of patience and letting go of the desire to see the
results right now.

We are also reminded here of *hupomone*, patience, which
we explored earlier in this book. Patience isn't just about being

comfortable with the slow passage of time, but about coming into a new relationship to time, God's time. Planning is a form of trying to control the speed at which things happen and the results. Yet most of the richness in our lives happens when we allow things to ripen slowly and organically.

Allow yourself to slow down and settle into a comfortable position. Breathe deeply and bring your awareness down to your heart center. Step into this inner sanctuary space. Abide for a while with the Beloved, breathing in love, breathing out peace.

Welcome in the presence of Abba John to the cave of your heart. Read through the story above again. Ask him for wisdom about diligence, patience, and attending to the slow ripening of things. Ask him what kept him going during those 1000+ days of commitment. Listen for the wisdom he has to offer.

Reflect on your own attachment to plans. What are the things in your life you wish would happen more quickly? Share some of this with him and listen for his response.

Ask Abba John to bless you with slowness and patience. He extends his hand to you and offers you a beautiful rosebud. As you gaze upon it, it opens slowly petal by petal until it is gloriously full and fragrant. You know this is a symbol for your journey.

Offer gratitude to him and gently return to the room you are in. Spend some time in reflection on your experience and encounter.

DAY 5: CONTEMPLATIVE WALK

PREPARE FOR YOUR contemplative walk once again by first centering and slowing down. Take the time you need to bring yourself as present as you can as you prepare to go on a walk without a destination. As you walk, stay alert for the shimmering moments around you and pause.

Pay special attention on your walk to how the world is ripening around you. Nature shows us examples of organic unfolding in every stage of that process from seed to fullness and fruition to release and decay.

As you discover these holy moments, pause and take in these visible signs of the ripening journey. Ask yourself how your own life is like each of these.

DAY 6: IMAGINATIVE PRAYER

I am the true vine, and my Father is the vinegrower.
He removes every branch in me that bears no fruit.
Every branch that bears fruit he prunes to make it
bear more fruit. You have already been cleansed by
the word that I have spoken to you. Abide in me as
I abide in you. Just as the branch cannot bear fruit
by itself unless it abides in the vine, neither can you
unless you abide in me. I am the vine; you are the
branches. Those who abide in me and I in them
bear much fruit, because apart from me you can do
nothing.

Jesus, the True Vine (John 15:1–5)

READ THE SCRIPTURE passage for this week once again. Enter into the story with all your senses awake and attuned. As Jesus teaches about vines, branches, and fruit, enter into a sensory experience of this. See, taste, smell, and feel the vines as they grow and reach and root down.

Enter into conversation with Jesus about the deeper meaning of this story. What wisdom does he have for your life right now? Engage in a dialogue with the vines, branches, and fruit each separately and then all in conversation with one another. See what these elements of the story reveal.

Move through the story again with a somatic awareness. What does being cleansed by the word feel like for you? What does the experience of abiding feel like in your body? In what ways does Jesus abide in you? Feel the difference between being a branch rooted in the true vine and one that has become disconnected from its source.

Listen for what the wind and the soil have to say too. How does the sun sweeten the fruit that is growing? Are there any places in the story that stir your curiosity?

Spend some time engaging on these various levels of conversation and the senses. Ask for the wisdom you seek. Write the story that emerges in the spaces between.

DAY 7: CREATIVE RITUAL OF BLOOMING

FOR YOUR RITUAL this week I invite you to plant a seed of some kind or get one of those lovely bulbs that bloom indoors like an amaryllis. If you choose a seed, you might select something that grows fairly quickly like marigolds. Get a small pot with potting soil and offer a prayer over this act of planting. Then let the journey of witnessing the unfolding and ripening of the seed into shoot into plant be a way of honoring the slow ripening of your own soul. When the plant is too big for the seed pot you will want to transfer it to a larger one.

I love amaryllis bulbs because the growth and flowering happens relatively quickly and offers a stunning display of petals when they open. Whichever plant you choose, again, let this process be a prayerful one. Find the right spot for the plant so you can see it on a daily basis. Bless it in each stage of its growth. Witness what happens each day. Offer a prayer on behalf of the bud, the petals opening, the face of the flower slowly revealed. As you witness this plant each day, ask what wisdom it has for the season of life you are in.

Reflection Questions

What is your own relationship to calendars, planning, deadlines, and to-do lists?

What are the ways you schedule your life that end up costing you or depleting you?

How do the seasons, with their own rhythms of unfolding and ripening, teach you about another way to be present to your life?

What do you discover about your true hunger when you let go of the need to control the direction and outcome of things?

—————— **CLOSING BLESSING** ——————

Ripening One,

dazzle us with the rhythm of your seasons

woven into all of Creation.

Help us to see how release and rest

are necessary for flowering and fruit.

Bring us reminders each day

of our own holy unfolding

from waking to working to playing to waning.

Release our grip from calendars and planners,

soften our need to make something happen,

to try to control the outcome,

and reveal your impulse arising in us

in a hundred different ways.

Guide our hearts and soften our impatience.

We celebrate this wild grace at work,

in its own time, its own tempo

inviting us into this sacred dance of trust.

Week 6

AN INVITATION TO FAST FROM CERTAINTY

EMBRACE MYSTERY AND WAITING

Week 6 Reflection

AS I SHARED in the introduction to our journey, John Cassian, one of the ancient desert fathers, describes three renunciations he says are required of all of us on the spiritual journey.

The first is our former way of life as we move closer to our heart's deep desires and true hungers.

The second is the inner practice of asceticism and letting go of our mindless thoughts that distract us from presence to the divine.

The third renunciation is to let go of our images of God—the idols we cling to so tightly—and to recognize that any image or pronouncement we can ever make about God is much too small to contain the divine. We experience this with the prevalent images of white Jesus which reinforces a system rooted in white supremacy. But we also experience it in more subtle ways when we imagine that God can only work in certain ways in our lives.

Even the word "God" is problematic because it carries with it so many interpretations and limits based on our cultural understandings. We are called to let go of "God" in the service of meeting the Great Mystery of the divine beyond our understanding. The search for the sacred always involves these layers of letting go.

We live in an age when fundamentalism has emerged as an overwhelming force in religious consciousness. In times that are chaotic and uncertain, our human minds grasp for a sense of control. One of the ways we try to make sense of things is to engage in black-and-white thinking. Establishing clear rules for how the world works, and who is inside and outside of God's sphere, is a way of coping with this felt loss of an anchor or shared cultural sense of meaning.

There is a beautiful quote in a journal entry dated December 2, 1851, from a book titled *Amiel's Journal* by Henri-Frederic Amiel:

> *Let mystery have its place in you; do not be always turning up your whole soil with the plowshare of self-examination but leave a little fallow corner in*

> *your heart ready for any seed the winds may bring,*
> *and reserve a nook of shadow for the passing bird;*
> *keep a place in your heart for the unexpected guests,*
> *an altar for an unknown God.*

I love this invitation to let mystery have a place within us. When we are on a spiritual path our temptation might be to plow up the fertile soil of our being with our self-examination and inquiry. We are called to leave some darkness for the seed, shadow for the bird, and an altar for the God we can only know dimly.

Amiel goes on to write: "If you are conscious of something new—thought or feeling, wakening in the depths of your being—do not be in a hurry to let in light upon it, to look at it; let the springing germ have the protection of being forgotten, hedge it round with quiet, and do not break in upon its darkness; let it take shape and grow . . . all conception should be enwrapped by the triple veil of modesty, silence and night."

Darkness is the place of conception, of new birthing. Mystery calls us into the silence and night so as to sit with the shape of things to come, rather than an examination of things as they are.

The *via negativa* or apophatic way in the Christian tradition, which means the way of unknowing, demands that we talk about God only in terms of negatives or what God is not. It helps to cleanse us of our idols. Alan Jones, in his book *Soul*

Making, writes, "We can only say that God is both unknowable and inexhaustible." To enter the unknown to meet the inexhaustible requires humility. It requires loosening of our attachment to images of who God is and how God works in the world. Ultimately, what the desert journey demands is that we let go of even this false idol and open ourselves to the God who is far more expansive than we can behold or imagine.

Letting go of our images of God can be terrifying. And often comes as the result of an experience of suffering in our lives, when our previous understanding is no longer adequate to give meaning to what has happened to us. When I was in my thirties and my mother suddenly died, I was thrust into the desert. All of my certainties about God and life were stripped away and I was left raw and frightened. Many people offered trite words and shallow comfort in my grief. They were not willing to sit with me in the darkness, but only hoped to rush me through to a place of light.

This is the mystical experience of the "dark night of the soul," when old convictions and conformities dissolve into nothingness and we are called to stand naked to the terror of the unknown. We must let the process move through us—one that is much greater than we can comprehend. We can never force our way back to the light. It is only in this place of absolute surrender that the new possibility can emerge. We don't just have one dark night in our lives, but again and again, as we are called to continue releasing the images we cling to so tightly.

Sheri Hostetler is a Mennonite poet whose poem "Instructions" begins with "Give up the world; give up self; finally, give up God." Her choice of words is certainly provocative, and when I read this poem in classes and on retreats, I encounter a wide range of reactions, from an audible sigh of relief to the anxious confusion over whether I am proposing a kind of atheism.

This is the call of the desert elders: to let go, let go, let go, and let go some more, on every level of our lives, to everything we cling to, including, or especially our ideas about God. As soon as our human minds begin to fashion categories, we risk making idols of them.

We let go of who we believe God to be and cultivate an openness to the One who is far beyond the horizons of our imagining. In the book of Job, God challenges Job's desire for understanding and asks, "Where were you when I laid the foundation of the earth?" (Job 38:4). God is never a set of concepts to be understood and grasped, but a relationship to encounter. In this way, the spiritual life is always a journey and in process. We do not let go once and for all but move through the layers of clinging in our lives until we are living more from our hearts than our minds. We do not arrive, but travel toward the horizon, realizing that it is always receding from our view.

Often, we meet this mystery in the place of our own unfulfilled longings. Howard Thurman writes about the patience of unanswered prayer:

> *it opens up before the mind the wide intensity of*
> *unfulfilled hopes, broken dreams and anguished*
> *denials. Who is there that has not carried at a*
> *central place in his concerns the persistent hunger,*
> *sometimes dull and quiet, sometimes feverish and*
> *angry, for something that has not come to pass.*

We may feel peace at times with these longings that seem to go unanswered, but more likely we seek and probe and try to find an answer. Thurman continues:

> *Slowly it may dawn upon the spirit that there is a*
> *special ministry of unfulfillment. It may be that the*
> *persistent hunger is an Angel of Light, carrying out a*
> *particular assignment in life.*

He suggests that considering this possibility of the desires and longings we have as its own kind of angel can facilitate us slowly relaxing all that we want to hold onto.

Sometimes, as we seek for a way forward, nature can reveal images that help us dwell in these in-between places of our lives. When I first moved to the Pacific Northwest United States in 2003, I fell in love with trails that run along the border spaces between forest and ocean. Walking these paths is like walking along the edges where two wild places meet, and in that space I encounter the wilderness within me. This landscape of earth and sea pressed against each other, wild against wild, speaks to something deep within me—that place where God's voice often whispers and sometimes roars. It reflects the landscape of my soul in a way that no other place had until I moved to Ireland and found a new landscape of wild edges. I somehow feel very much at home in this place of borders.

We often try to domesticate God and to make spirituality about happiness or feeling good. We try and tie things up in neat packages. The spiritual journey is about none of these. It demands something of us and calls us to stand in uncomfortable places while the deserts of our lives strip away ego and power and identity. It calls us to embrace the God of wild borderlands.

Lent is in part about dwelling in the border spaces of life and recognizing those places and experiences that do not offer us easy answers, those fierce edges of life where things are not as clear-cut as I hope for them to be. There is beauty in the border spaces, those places of ambiguity and mystery. In Esther de Waal's rich little book *To Pause at the Threshold: Reflections on Living on the Border*, she writes that the ability to live with uncertainty requires courage and the need to ask questions over finding answers. We are called to hold the space for mystery within me.

In *Living on the Border of the Holy: Renewing the Priesthood of All*, William Countryman writes that this border country is one we all carry within us. There is a fault line running down the middle of our lives that connects our ordinary reality with its deeper roots. The border country, he argues, is what gives our lives meaning:

> *This border country is a place of intense vitality. It*
> *does not so much draw us away from the everyday*
> *world as it plunges us deeper into a reality of which*
> *the everyday world is like the surface. . . . To live*
> *there for a while is like having the veils pulled away.*

Threshold space opens us up to life that is vital, intense, and filled with unknowns. Borders and edges are the places of transformation, transformation that makes demands of us. Jesus's journey in the desert was a willingness to dwell in the border space of that landscape and the walk through Holy Week often fills us with more questions than answers.

This week I invite you to fast from the places in your life where you crave certainty and sure outcomes and release them to the great Mystery. Celebrate a God who is infinitely larger than your imagination and rest in the possibilities that affords.

Daily Practices

DAY 1: *LECTIO DIVINA*

> *Now there was a garden in the place where [Jesus]*
> *was crucified, and in the garden there was a new*
> *tomb in which no one had ever been laid. And so,*
> *because it was the Jewish day of Preparation, and*
> *the tomb was nearby, they laid Jesus there.*
>   *Laying the Body in the Tomb (John 19:41–42)*

HOLY WEEK INVITES us into a world full of betrayal, abandonment, mockery, violence, and ultimately death. The Triduum, those three sacred days that constitute one unfolding liturgy in the Christian church, call us to experience communion, loss, and the border spaces of unknowing. Holy Saturday is an invitation to make a conscious passage through the liminal realm of in-between.

I love the wide space of Holy Saturday that lingers between the suffering and death of Jesus on Friday and the vigil Saturday night proclaiming the return of the Easter fire. For me, Holy Saturday evokes much about the human condition—the ways we are called to let go of things or people, identities or securities, and then wonder what will rise up out of the ashes of our lives. The suffering that we experience because of pain or grief or great sorrow, and we don't know if we will ever grasp joy again. Our lives are full of Holy Saturday experiences, suspended in that space between loss and hope.

In their book *The Last Week: What the Gospels Really Teach about Jesus's Final Days in Jerusalem*, Marcus Borg and John Dominic Crossan write:

> *Easter completes the archetypal pattern at the center of the Christian life: death and resurrection, crucifixion and vindication. Both parts of this pattern are essential: death and resurrection, crucifixion and vindication. When one is emphasized over the other distortion is the result. The two must be affirmed equally.*

Before we rush to resurrection we must dwell fully in the space of unknowing, of holding death and life in tension with each other, to experience that liminal place so that we become familiar with its landscape and one day might accompany others who find themselves there and similarly disoriented. The wisdom of the Triduum is that we must be fully present to both the starkness of Friday and to the Saturday space between, before we can really experience the resurrection. We must know the terrible experience of loss wrought again and again in our world so that when the promise of new life dawns we can let it enter into us fully in the space carved by loss. As the great poet of Hafiz reminds us, we must let our loneliness "cut more deep" and "season" us, so that we are reminded of our absolute dependence on the Source of all.

Even as much of our lives are spent in Holy Saturday places, we spend so much energy resisting, longing for resolution and closure. Our practice as we approach this day is to really enter into the liminal zone, to be present to it with every cell of our being.

Pray with this passage and enter into the unknown of the tomb. Listen for the word or phrase, letting it unfold in your imagination. Listen for the invitation mystery has for you. Rest into silence.

DAY 2: BREATH PRAYER—I REST INTO MYSTERY

OUR BREATH CAN again be an ally in this practice of fasting from certainty and learning to rest more deeply into mystery. Begin by slowing your breath and noticing the four moments of breath: inhale, the fullness between, exhale, the emptiness between. These form a kind of parallel to the seasons of spring, summer, autumn, and winter, with the exhale reflecting autumn's release, and the emptiness of the breath between exhale and the next inhale holding the energies of winter's stillness, emptiness, and mystery. Move through a few breath cycles, paying special attention to that moment of emptiness.

Then begin to bring in your breath prayer:

Breathe in: I rest

Breathe out: Into mystery

As you inhale, whisper "I rest" and feel yourself opening to the rest that mystery invites us into—resting our mind, our thoughts, our gaze, our hands, our hearts. Invite your inhale to bathe each of these parts with healing breath.

As you exhale, whisper "into mystery," and imagine what mystery looks like to you. Is it the fertile dark earth? Is it the night sky? Is it being cozied in bed under blankets and preparing for sleep? See if you can find a positive association with mystery and bring that image into your prayer if it is helpful.

DAY 3: *VISIO DIVINA*

I INVITE YOU to pray with the block print image by artist Kreg Yingst that opens this chapter. Begin by slowing yourself down and dropping your awareness into your heart center. Bring a soft gaze to the image and let your eyes wander slowly around it.

Notice the body of Jesus wrapped in linen, the wounds in his hands and feet. See the halo of light around his head and his posture of repose in the tomb. Notice the black that forms negative space around the image.

Take in the stairs on the left side and the rays of light at the top of the frame. Let your eyes journey around the two frames within the image, both in the space around and in the spaces within.

As you continue to gaze, see if anything expands or shifts. What do you see after spending time with the images? What feelings and memories are stirred?

Listen for any sense of invitation that is arising in this prayer experience. Make space for the call to a new awareness. How does this image support me in the call to fast from certainty and embrace mystery?

Rest for a few moments in stillness, with gratitude for whatever has come. After a time in silence, gaze one more time on the image and see if anything else is sparked in your heart. How does this image support you in the call to fast from certainty and embrace mystery? Allow some time to journal or draw your responses.

DAY 4: MEDITATION WITH THE DESERT ELDERS

> *One day some old men came to see Abba Anthony.*
> *In the midst of them was Abba Joseph. Wanting*
> *to test them, the old man suggested a text from the*
> *Scriptures, and, beginning with the youngest, he*
> *asked them what it meant. Each gave his opinion as*
> *he was able. But to each one the old man said, "You*
> *have not understood it." Last of all he said to Abba*
> *Joseph, "How would you explain this saying?" and*
> *he replied, "I do not know." Then Abba Anthony*
> *said, "Indeed, Abba Joseph has found the way, for he*
> *has said: 'I do not know.'" (Anthony 17)*

THIS PATH OF unknowing is at the heart of desert spirituality. We release everything we think we know to rest in the source of all truth. We even move toward letting go of our ideas about God. Simone Weil tells us that "there are two atheisms of which one is a purification of the notion of God." Purification of God means surrendering all the images that confine the sacred to certain people or places or moments. The call of the desert is to let go, let go, let go, and let go some more, on every level of our lives. The desert has the power to open our hearts to what our minds cannot understand.

Read this story through again and let that phrase, "I do not know," echo in your heart as you slow down your breathing and rest into the arms of the Divine. Drop your awareness into the cave of your heart and rest there for a few breaths.

Welcome in again the presence of Abba Anthony—as we meditated with him once before. Ask him for wisdom about letting go of certainty. Listen to his guidance for how to be with the mystery of things.

Share anything in your heart you are struggling with in terms of not knowing. See as Abba Anthony extends a stone to you. It is a stone local to your geology and you marvel for a moment as you can see the millions of years that went into forming it.

Offer gratitude for the abba's presence and return gently to the room you are in. Allow some time for reflection.

DAY 5: CONTEMPLATIVE WALK—WALK WITH MYSTERY

IF YOU ARE able, walk in an edge space like a shoreline or the edge of a woodland. An alternative is to climb a local hill or mountain as a border place between heaven and earth. As you walk, open your heart to mystery. Allow this borderland to speak to you of liminality, of those moments in between when we lose our certainty about things and open to something different. Be present to threshold places along the way, like walking between two trees or two stones.

Stay attentive to the things you encounter that beckon you toward questions and not knowing, instead of certainty. Kindle your curiosity about the world around you. What are the symbols of mystery being offered from nature? See if there is a stone that calls to you and speaks of endurance and ancient wisdom. Ask nature to reveal to you the heart of mystery and how to stay present to it.

If you have your camera with you, be open to receiving images of mystery. What does it look like? Feel like? Sound like? Smell like?

When you return allow some time to sit in silence with what has unfolded. Ask to receive the nourishment you need from this journey to help sustain you.

DAY 6: IMAGINATIVE PRAYER

> *Now there was a garden in the place where [Jesus]*
> *was crucified, and in the garden there was a new*
> *tomb in which no one had ever been laid. And so,*
> *because it was the Jewish day of Preparation, and*
> *the tomb was nearby, they laid Jesus there.*
> Laying the Body in the Tomb (John 19:41–42)

READ THE SCRIPTURE passage for this week again. Step into this garden where the new tomb is. Be in the scene as the others take Jesus down from the cross and prepare to lay him there before the Sabbath begins. Help carry the weight of his body.

Wander through the garden, taking in what is growing there, the scents, the sights. Touch the plants bringing life to this space. Look and listen for birds and other creatures.

Stand by the tomb as the mourners lay Jesus's body to rest. Rest in the silence with them for a while. When the time feels right, consider engaging in conversation with one or more people there. Ask them what they have seen, how they feel, what they are going to do now. Have a dialogue with the garden, the plant life, the tomb itself, Jesus's body.

Sit inside the tomb for a period of time. Rest into the waiting. Recognize those places in your own life where you await new life.

Write a story from this place. Listen to what is unfolding in your heart and put it on paper or do some expressive drawing.

DAY 7: CREATIVE RITUAL OF HOLY DARKNESS

I INVITE YOU into a ritual of embracing the darkness. You will need a space where you can turn out the lights and be in the dark, so either at night or in a room where you can block out daylight from windows.

Make some time on Holy Saturday to sit with all of the paradoxes of life. Bring yourself as fully present as you can to the discomfort of the experience. Rest in the space of waiting and unknowing and resist trying to come up with neat answers or resolutions.

Sit in your prayer space with a lit candle. Meditate on the flame for a few minutes as you settle into the experience. Notice how it flickers and dances. See the shapes of things in the room and how they are revealed through the flame.

Take some nice slow, deep breaths and, when you are ready, extinguish the flame on the candle. Sit in the darkness, breathing and resting, letting it embrace you.

Imagine yourself on a wild border or standing on a threshold, knowing that you cannot fully embrace what is on the other side until you have let this place shape and form your heart. When you notice your attention drifting or your mind starting to analyze, return to your breath and the present moment. Allow yourself to feel whatever arises in this space. Honor the mystery.

Ask what are the places in your life where you are longing for clear answers? See if you can offer these over to the sacred darkness. Imagine planting them like tiny seeds in the fertile black soil.

You might play a piece of music if that helps you to become more fully present. Maybe instrumental music or a piece of music like Loreena McKennitt's song "Dark Night of the Soul," which can be found in an online search and is an adaptation of the prayer of John of the Cross. You might play the song and then rest into silence.

Movement practice can also be helpful in helping us to dwell in a place without words. After you have rested in the darkness for a while, light your candle again, and let your body move into different shapes or gestures, holding each one for a few breaths. You are not directing your body but listening for what movements are arising in the moment. This is a way of honoring your intuitive wisdom where mystery lives.

Reflection Questions

What are the aspects of your life where you crave certainty?

Has there ever been a time of your life when what unfolded
was even better than what you could have imagined?

As you ponder the gifts of mystery, what true hunger do you
discover?

CLOSING BLESSING

God of Holy Darkness,

be with us in our desire to know,

in the ache to be certain,

in the longing for assurance.

Sit with us in the long quiet nights,

hold us in our winter seasons.

Wrap us in the grace of mystery,

finding comfort in this mantle

of unknowing as we rest our thoughts.

Remind us of how everything emerges

from the black fertile womb space

of new beginnings, from the rich soil

where seeds are planted.

Sustain us in the times when

not knowing is painful, fearful, anguished.

Abide with us in the space

of sacred Mystery, bring comfort,

whisper words of love to us in the silence.

Living the Wisdom Forward

Resurrection Blessings

WHEN WE MAKE the journey through the heart of the desert, allowing the excess to be stripped away, we hope to arrive on the other side with more capacity for what is vital, alive, and precious in our lives.

This commitment to different ways of fasting through Lent has hopefully cleared out some inner spaciousness within us so that our grasping has softened and our spirits can breathe more fully.

In these weeks we have explored a fast from consumption to embrace simplicity, from distraction to embrace presence, from anxiety to embrace trust in abundance, from rushing to embrace slowness, from strength to embrace vulnerability, from planning to embrace ripening, and from certainty to embrace mystery. Is there one of these that has shimmered the most brightly for you? Felt the most essential for the ongoing development of your spiritual journey and growing intimacy with the divine?

There is a beautiful emphasis on heightened spiritual practice for Lent. But as we enter the season of Easter, we are given a fifty-day journey through the practice of resurrection. Now that we have fasted and yielded and let go, we can ask during the season of Easter, What do I long to fully embrace? We can feast—on good and nourishing food, on love and friendship, on creativity. When Jesus appears in the resurrection narratives of the gospels it is in an embodied way—inviting the disciples to touch his wounds, a gathered abundance of so many fish the disciples' nets were overflowing, and his breathing out on his followers, blessing and sending with his breath.

The purpose of our fasting is not for its own sake. It is to make room for the greater joy and aliveness that is promised to us. Feasting gains its meaning and significance through fasting, through meditating on what it means to go without. Fasting helps us connect to our true hunger.

What are the true hungers you have discovered on this pilgrimage?

Commitment to Ongoing Practice: Three Suggestions

A Daily Meditation

I return here to this saying that I introduced early on in the book:

> *(Abba Poemen) said, "Do not give your heart to that which does not satisfy your heart." (Poemen 80)*

A very simple practice at the end of each day can be an adapted Examen prayer (inspired by Ignatius of Loyola) where you reflect on the previous twenty-four hours and ask yourself:

> *What truly nourished me?*
> *What satisfied my deep hunger?*
> *When did I feel satisfied at the level of soul?*

Allow time to remember these experiences and bring gratitude for these moments. Choose one in particular to especially savor and remember how it felt in your body and heart. Soak in that grace.

Then reflect again on the previous day and ask yourself:

> *What depleted me?*
> *What did not feel satisfying?*
> *What distracted me or exhausted me?*

Bring compassion for the moments that arise in your memory and forgiveness to yourself if that feels appropriate. Make a commitment to begin again and nourish yourself as well as you can going forward.

You could also bring this to a breath prayer practice.

> *On the inhale, say: Give my heart*
> *nourishment*
> *On the exhale, say: Release what depletes*

I recommend closing with some time to journal. Keeping track of what arises in this prayer can be a powerful act of discernment of the things in your life that are life-giving and those that are life-draining.

Ask the Desert Elders

We have engaged in a series of contemplative practices during this time of Lenten retreat. If you have found a sacred rhythm nourishing, consider how you might adapt this rhythm to your life going forward. Which of the practices felt most life-giving that you want to continue? Which practices best helped you to identify what you needed to release and embrace?

Invite in one of the desert elders to offer you wisdom for this discernment. Consider this story from Abba Poemen:

> *Abba Poemen said, "The nature of water is soft,*
> *that of stone is hard; but if a bottle is hung above*
> *the stone, allowing the water to fall drop by drop, it*
> *wears away the stone. So it is with the word of God;*
> *it is soft and our heart is hard, but the (person) who*
> *hears the word of God often, opens his (or her) heart*
> *to God." (Poemen 183)*

You might want to spend some time with Abba Poemen or any of the other desert elders who you sat with in meditation. Center yourself and drop into the sanctuary of your heart.

Invite in the desert mothers and fathers to be with you and to bless you on this threshold of a new season.

Meditate with the image of the water wearing away the stone. Consider the practices you have engaged in. Which of them had the greatest effect of softening your heart?

Remember the gifts you were given each week from the desert monks at the end of your meditation times together: a clay bowl, a beeswax candle, a pomegranate, a spiral shell, a small glass vial, a rosebud, and a stone. If you haven't yet, you might want to try collecting physical representations of these symbols and put them on a home altar as a reminder of the resources you have to support you going forward.

Always Begin Again

The desert monks tried to practice what the Buddhists call "beginner's mind." In his Rule, Benedict describes it as a "little Rule for beginners." Remembering this we are less likely to get caught up in our own hubris about the spiritual life. The desert monks invite us again and again to commit to our spiritual practice and path. Abba Poemen encourages us to make a new beginning each day as well:

> *Abba Poemen said about Abba Pior that every single day he made a fresh beginning.*

This is the essence of humility—to remember that we are always beginning in the spiritual life. The moment we think that we have it all figured out, the further we are from the spiritual path. Conversely, when we think we have fallen away too far to return, we have doomed ourselves to never try at all.

In *Listen to the Desert*, Gregory Mayers writes about the times we want to give up our spiritual practice, especially through boredom, and how these times are when the practice is purifying us and our attachments to how prayer should be. The desert calls us over and over to commitment: "There are only three stages to this work: to be a beginner, to be more of a beginner, and to be only a beginner."

> *Abba Abraham told of a man of Scetis who was a scribe and did not eat bread. A brother came to beg him to copy a book. The old man whose spirit was engaged in contemplation, wrote, omitting some phrases and with no punctuation. The brother, taking the book and wishing to punctuate it, noticed that words were missing. So he said to the old man, "Abba, there are some phrases missing." The old man said to him, "Go, and practice first that which is written, then come back and I will write the rest."*
> *(Abraham 3)*

I love this story about receiving a book with missing words and punctuation. "Go, and practice first that which is written," says Abba Abraham. Do not be impatient, but deepen into the wisdom already offered here. I am reminded that I already know everything I need in this moment to live fully. There is no other book or experience that will make me more complete. Once it has been integrated through practice I will naturally be drawn to seek more; that is the nature of a curious and hungry heart. But again, the caution is to not let the words in a book become a substitute for my own deep knowing.

What are the true hungers you have discovered? Go and nourish those well. Let this Easter be a true practice of resurrection flowing from the fasts you have taken on. Let yourself be filled with new life.

—— CLOSING BLESSING ——

This blessing has sat with you
in your hunger and fullness,
has held the space opening inside of you
no longer filled with busyness and rushing,
no longer walled off with strength and noise,
it has watched as the space left by fasting
has been filled with paint of vibrant hues:
love, kindness, slowness, presence, trust, mystery.

This blessing is a burst of new life
come to remind you of the graces that await
when you commit to the hard road of practice,
it has sat with you in waiting rooms
and wiped the sweat from your brow,
the tears from your cheeks,
and now it arrives like a rain shower after drought.

This blessing is a bouquet of daffodils,
golden light, fragrant with sunshine
shimmering with the promise of spring.

This blessing sits at the table with you,

asks, What is necessary and essential?

What can be released, set sail on the breeze?

It holds your hands as you open them slowly,

releasing your grip on all you have been clinging

so tightly to, it kisses your palms as you soften them.

This blessing calls you to embody

this resurrection being celebrated,

feel yourself deeply nourished,

feel all your true hungers satisfied.

Notes

Introduction

". . . 'that contemplation can occur anywhere. . ." Barbara Holmes, *Joy Unspeakable*, 2nd ed. (Minneapolis: Fortress Press, 2017), xxix.

". . . 'There are many who live in the mountains. . ." Benedicta Ward, SLG, trans., *The Sayings of the Desert Fathers* (Collegeville, MN: Cistercian Publications, 1975), 234.

"Today's wilderness can be found. . ." Holmes, *Joy Unspeakable*, 11.

"The Hebrews, the Aramaeans, the Arabs, . . ." Thomas Ryan, CSP, *The Sacred Art of Fasting* (Woodstock, VT: Skylight Paths), 13.

"Fasting as a religious act. . ." Ryan, *The Sacred Art of Fasting*, 163.

"One of the early teachings of the Christian church I find. . ." Margaret Funk, *Thoughts Matter* (Collegeville, MN: Liturgical Press, 2013), 9.

"Now I am revealing new things to you, . . ." Jerusalem Bible
     translation.

". . . When St. Benedict begins his Rule, he invites us. . ."
     Timothy Fry, trans., *The Rule of Benedict in English* (Col-
     legeville, MN: Liturgical Press, 1981), 15.

"For the early Hebrews, . . ." Norvene Vest, *Gathered in the
     Word* (Nashville, TN: Upper Room, 2019), 34–35.

"Abba Daniel used to tell how. . ." Ward, *The Sayings of the
     Desert Fathers*, 11.

"To live without speaking is better. . ." Ward, 98.

"A brother renounced the world. . ." Ward, 5.

"One day one of the young men asked him. . ." Alan Jones,
     Soul Making: The Desert Way of Spirituality (New York:
     HarperOne, 1989), 16.

"(Amma Theodora) also said that neither asceticism, . . ."
     Ward, *The Sayings of the Desert Fathers*, 84.

". . . 'Spiritual practices,' he writes, . . ." Tyler Sit, *Staying
     Awake: The Gospel for Changemakers* (Danvers, MA: Chal-
     ice Press, 2021), 65–66.

"A helpful place to begin is. . ." This section is adapted from
     Christine Valters Paintner, *Lectio Divina—The Sacred Art:
     Transforming Words and Images into Heart-Centered Prayer*
     (Woodstock, VT: Skylight Paths, 2011). Used by permis-
     sion of SkyLight Paths Publishing.

"Now I am revealing new things to you, . . ." Jerusalem Bible
     translation.

"Our breath is such an intimate companion. . . ." This section
     is adapted from Christine Valters Paintner, *Breath Prayer:
     An Ancient Practice for the Everyday Sacred* (Minneapolis:
     Broadleaf Books, 2021). Used by permission.

". . . St. Hesychios the Priest writes: "let the name of Jesus. . ."" St. Hesychios the Priest, I, *On Watchfulness and Holiness*, sec. 100. Quoted in *Philokalia—The Eastern Christian Spiritual Texts* (Woodstock, VT: SkyLight Paths, 2006), Kindle.

". . . 'the sustainer of life and also the vehicle for entry into the contemplative center. . . .'" Holmes, *Joy Unspeakable*, 149.

"The four movements of *lectio* we explored earlier. . ." This section is adapted from Christine Valters Paintner, *Eyes of the Heart: Photography as a Christian Contemplative Practice* (Notre Dame, IN: Ave Maria Press, 2013).

"It would perhaps be too much to say that the world needs. . ." Thomas Merton, *The Wisdom of the Desert* (New York: New Directions, 1960), 23.

". . . 'The sanctified imagination is the fertile creative space. . .'" Wilda Gafney, *Womanist Midrash* (Louisville, KY: Westminster John Knox Press, 2017), 3.

". . . 'Think of the ways that questions illuminate. . .'" Phil Cousineau, *The Art of Pilgrimage* (San Francisco: Conari Press, 2021), 24.

"I want to beg you, as much as I can, . . ." Rainer Maria Rilke, *Letters to a Young Poet*, trans. M. D. Herter Norton (New York: W. W. Norton, 1934), 27.

". . . 'Let us get up then, at long last, . . .'" Fry, *Rule of Benedict*, 16.

"All of this is mere verbiage. . ." Cyprian Consiglio, *Prayer in the Cave of the Heart: The Universal Call to Contemplation* (Collegeville, MN: Liturgical Press, 2010), x–xi.

"I asked myself this question: What if all my previous prayers. . ." Sophfronia Scott, *The Seeker and the Monk* (Minneapolis: Broadleaf Books, 2021), 123.

Ash Wednesday Week

". . . 'I put my foot out to ascend the ladder, . . ." Ward, *The Sayings of the Desert Fathers*, 230.

". . . 'Facing death gives our loving force, clarity, . . ." Jones, *Soul Making*, 60.

". . . '"Our bodies are made of the burned-out embers of stars. . ." Karel Schrijver and Iris Schrijver, *Living with the Stars: How the Human Body Is Connected to the Life Cycles of the Earth, the Planets, and the Stars* (Oxford: Oxford University Press, 2015), 1.

". . . 'we are, indeed, stardust, in a very literal sense. . . ." Schrijver and Schrijver, *Living with the Stars*, 8–9.

". . . Abba Daniel used to say, "He lived with us many a long year. . ." Ward, *The Sayings of the Desert Fathers*, 11.

Week 1

". . . 'A brother came to Scetis to visit Abba Moses. . ." Ward, *The Sayings of the Desert Fathers*, 139.

"Abba Moses' 'cell' is a metaphor. . ." Gregory Mayers, *Listen to the Desert: Secrets of Spiritual Maturity from the Desert Fathers and Mothers* (Chicago: ACTA Publications, 2014), 7.

". . . 'Just as fish die . . ." Ward, *The Sayings of the Desert Fathers*, 3.

". . . 'We carry ourselves wherever we go. . ." Laura Swan, *Forgotten Desert Mothers: Sayings, Lives, and Stories of Early*

Christian Women, 1st ed. (New York: Paulist Press, 2001), 35.

"There was a monk, . . ." Ward, *The Sayings of the Desert Fathers*, 84.

". . . 'It is both a quest. . ." Therese Taylor-Stinson, *Walking the Way of Harriet Tubman: Public Mystic & Freedom Fighter* (Minneapolis: Broadleaf Books, 2023), 132.

". . . 'For me, most simply, contemplative spirituality is a fidelity. . ." Cole Arthur Riley, *This Here Flesh: Spirituality, Liberation and the Stories that Make Us* (London: Hodder & Stoughton, 2022), x.

". . . 'We have found ourselves too busy for beauty. . . ." Riley, *This Here Flesh*, 38–39.

"Amma Syncletica said, 'There are many who live in the mountains. . ." Ward, *The Sayings of the Desert Fathers*, 234.

Week 2

"Nothing happens, which is enough to frighten. . ." Robert Johnson, *The Fisher King and the Handless Maiden* (New York: HarperOne, 1995), 93.

". . . 'desperate and valid question. . ." Tricia Hersey, *Rest Is Resistance: A Manifesto* (New York: Little, Brown, 2022), 16.

". . . 'Rest disrupts and makes space. . ." Hersey, *Rest Is Resistance*, 161.

". . . Walter Brueggemann, in his wonderful book *Sabbath as Resistance*, . . ." Walter Brueggemann, *Sabbath as Resistance: Saying No to the Culture of Now* (Louisville, KY: Westminster John Knox Press, 2017), xii.

". . . we are so beholden to 'accomplishing and achieving and possessing' . . ." Brueggemann, *Sabbath as Resistance*, xiv.

". . . 'Here is an unspeakable secret. . .'" Thomas Merton, *Conjectures of a Guilty Bystander* (New York: Image Books, 2009), 128.

". . . 'I felt something open up in my whole being. . . .'" Scott, *Seeker and the Monk*, 4.

". . . 'What if what is central to God's reality. . .'" Makoto Fujimura, *Art + Faith: A Theology of Making* (New Haven, CT: Yale University Press, 2021), 87.

"(Abba Poemen) said, 'Do not give your heart to that. . .'" Ward, *The Sayings of the Desert Fathers*, 178.

Week 3

"Our societies and communities have a way of grinding up. . ." Riley, *This Here Flesh*, 11.

". . . I love this image of those who are unable to 'do'. . ." Hersey, *Rest Is Resistance*, 149.

". . . 'One could not begin the cultivation of the prayer life. . .'" Howard Thurman, *Meditations of the Heart* (Boston: Beacon Press, 1999), 27.

". . . 'The moment of pause, the point of rest, . . .'" Thurman, *Meditations of the Heart*, 29.

"God discovered a point at which, even in Her infinite expansiveness, . . ." Sit, *Staying Awake*, 113.

"A hunter in the desert saw Abba Anthony enjoying himself. . ." Ward, *The Sayings of the Desert Fathers*, 3–4.

Week 4

". . . 'Tears and weeping indicate a significant frontier. . .'" John Chryssavgis, *In the Heart of the Desert: The Spirituality of the Desert Fathers and Mothers* (Bloomington: World Wisdom, 2008), 48.

". . . 'when we men weaponize stereotypes of masculinity. . ."
Sit, *Staying Awake*, 10.

"It was said of (Abba Arsenius) that he had a hollow in his chest. . ." Ward, *The Sayings of the Desert Fathers*, 18.

Week 5

"It was said of Abba Agathon that for three years he lived with a stone in his mouth, . . ." Ward, *The Sayings of the Desert Fathers*, 22.

"Interior solitude is impossible for them. . . ." Thomas Merton, *New Seeds of Contemplation* (New York: New Directions, 2007), 83.

". . . 'Connecting to divine spirit requires surrender. . . ." Scott, *The Seeker and the Monk*, 56.

". . . 'Great Mystery unscrews the tight lids of certainty. . ." Randy Woodley, *Becoming Rooted: One Hundred Days of Reconnecting with Sacred Earth* (Minneapolis: Broadleaf Books, 2022), 16.

"It was said of Abba John that he withdrew and lived in the desert at Scetis. . ." Ward, *The Sayings of the Desert Fathers*, 85–86.

Week 6

"Let mystery have its place in you. . ." Henri-Frederic Amiel, *Amiel's Journal: The Journal Intime of Henri-Frederic Amiel* (London: Wentworth Press, 2019), 91.

"... 'We can only say that God is both unknowable and inexhaustible.'..." Jones, *Soul Making*, 26.

"... 'Give up the world; give up self...'" Sheri Hostetler, "Instructions," in *A Cappella: Mennonite Voices in Poetry* (Iowa City: University of Iowa Press, 2003), 126.

"it opens up before the mind the wide intensity of unfulfilled hopes,..." Thurman, *Meditations of the Heart*, 56.

"Slowly it may dawn upon the spirit..." Thurman, 57.

"... In Esther de Waal's rich little book *To Pause at the Threshold*..." Esther de Waal, *To Pause at the Threshold: Reflections on Living on the Border* (New York: Morehouse Publishing, 2004), 90.

"This border country is a place of intense vitality...." William Countryman, *Living on the Border of the Holy: Renewing the Priesthood of All* (New York: Morehouse Publishing, 1999), 11.

"Easter completes the archetypal pattern at the center of the Christian life..." Marcus Borg and John Dominic Crossan, *The Last Week: What the Gospels Really Teach about Jesus's Final Days in Jerusalem* (New York: HarperOne, 2007), 209.

"... As the great poet of Hafiz reminds us,..." Daniel Ladinsky, *The Gift: Poems by Hafiz, the Great Sufi Master* (New York: Penguin, 1999), 277.

"One day some old men came to see Abba Anthony...." Ward, *The Sayings of the Desert Fathers*, 4.

"... Simone Weil tells us that 'there are two atheisms...'" Quoted in Jones, *Soul Making*, 9.

Living the Wisdom Forward

"(Abba Poemen) said, "Do not give your heart..." Ward, *The Sayings of the Desert Fathers*, 178.

"Abba Poemen said, 'The nature of water is soft, . . .'" Ward,
192–93.

". . . In his Rule, Benedict describes it as. . ." Fry, *Rule of Benedict*, 73:8

"Abba Poemen said about Abba Pior that every single day. . ."
Quoted in David G. R. Keller, *Oasis of Wisdom: The World of the Desert Fathers and Mothers* (Collegeville, MN: Liturgical Press, 2005), 139.

". . . 'There are only three stages to this work. . ." Mayers,
Listen to the Desert, 30.

"Abba Abraham told of a man of Scetis who was a scribe. . ."
Ward, *The Sayings of the Desert Fathers*, 34.